POETRY AS
EXPERIENCE

MERIDIAN

Crossing Aesthetics

Werner Hamacher

& David E. Wellbery

Editors

Translated by
Andrea Tarnowski

*Stanford
University
Press*

---

*Stanford
California*

POETRY AS
EXPERIENCE

Philippe Lacoue-Labarthe

Poetry as Experience
was originally published in French in 1986
under the title *La poésie comme expérience*
©1986 by Christian Bourgois Editeur.

Assistance for the translation was provided by the
French Ministry of Culture.

Stanford University Press
Stanford, California

©1999 by the Board of Trustees
of the Leland Stanford Junior University

Printed in the United States of America

CIP data appear at the end of the book

Contents

A Note on Citation   ix

PART I: TWO POEMS BY PAUL CELAN   I

PART II: REMEMBERING DATES   39

§ 1 Catastrophe   41

§ 2 Prayer   71

§ 3 Sublime   87

§ 4 Hagiography   92

§ 5 The Power of Naming   95

§ 6 Pain   98

§ 7 Ecstasy   102

§ 8 Vertigo   104

§ 9 Blindness   106

Contents

§ 10 *Lied*   107

§ 11 Sky   111

§ 12 The Unforgivable   122

Notes   127

Works Cited   141

A Note on Citation

The abbreviation *GW* designates Paul Celan's *Gesammelte Werke*; *SW* designates Friedrich Hölderlin's *Sämtliche Werke*.

POETRY AS
EXPERIENCE

P A R T   O N E

Two Poems by Paul Celan

Expand art?
No. But accompany art into your own unique
place of no escape. And set yourself free.

"The Meridian"[1]

Here are two poems by Paul Celan:

TÜBINGEN, JÄNNER

Zur Blindheit über-
redete Augen.
Ihre—"ein
Rätsel ist Rein-
entsprungenes"—, ihre
Erinnerung an
schwimmende Hölderlintürme, möwen-
umschwirrt.

Besuche ertrunkener Schreiner bei
diesen
tauchenden Worten:

Käme,
käme ein Mensch,
käme ein Mensch zur Welt, heute, mit
dem Lichtbart der
Patriarchen: er dürfte,
spräch er von dieser
Zeit, er
dürfte

nur lallen und lallen,
immer-, immer-
zuzu.

("Pallaksch. Pallaksch.")

TÜBINGEN, JANUARY

Eyes talked into
blindness.
Their—"an enigma is
the purely
originated"—, their
memory of
Hölderlin towers afloat, circled
by whirring gulls.

Visits of drowned joiners to
these
submerging words:

Should,
should a man,
should a man come into the world, today, with
the shining beard of the
patriarchs: he could,
if he spoke of this
time, he
could
only babble and babble
over, over
againagain.

("Pallaksh. Pallaksh.")[2]

TODTNAUBERG

Arnika, Augentrost, der
Trunk aus dem Brunnen mit dem
Sternwürfel drauf,

in der
Hütte,

die in das Buch
—wessen Namen nahms auf
vor dem meinen?—
die in dies Buch
geschriebene Zeile von
einer Hoffnung, heute,
auf eines Denkenden
kommendes
Wort
im Herzen,

Waldwasen, uneingeebnet,
Orchis und Orchis, einzeln,

Krudes, später, im Fahren,
deutlich,

der uns fährt, der Mensch,
der's mit anhört,

die halb-
beschrittenen Knüppel-
pfade im Hochmoor,

Feuchtes,
viel.

TODTNAUBERG

Arnica, eyebright, the
draft from the well with the
starred die above it,

in the
hut,

the line
—whose name did the book
register before mine?—
the line inscribed
in that book about
a hope, today,
of a thinking man's

coming
word
in the heart,

woodland sward, unlevelled,
orchid and orchid, single,

coarse stuff, later, clear
in passing,

he who drives us, the man,
who listens in,

the half-
trodden wretched
tracks through the high moors,

dampness,
much.[3]

These two poems are well known; each of them has been translated into French at least twice. The first, which is part of the *Niemandsrose* collection (1963), was initially translated by André du
Bouchet (appearing in *L'Ephémère* 7, and then in *Strette*, published
by Mercure de France in 1971) before figuring in the complete edition of *La rose de personne*, edited by Martine Broda (Le Nouveau
Commerce, 1979). The second, issued on its own in 1968 and then
republished in *Lichtzwang* in July 1970, two or three months after
Celan's death, was translated by Jean Daive as early as 1970, and
then, several years later, by André du Bouchet (*Poèmes de Paul
Celan*, Clivages, 1978). Other published versions of these poems
may exist.[4]

It is obvious that the titles of both are places: Tübingen, Todtnauberg. The poems seem, in each case, to commemorate a visit.
But it is also obvious that these place names can additionally, even
primarily, be names of people. Whatever trope we use, the indica-
tions, the quotations, the allusions are all perfectly clear; and in any
case, we already know that Tübingen is Hölderlin, and Todtnauberg, Heidegger. I don't imagine it would be very useful to
stress the reasons that prompt us today (*heute*: each poem includes

the word) to associate the two poems. For everyone who is, as we
say, "concerned about our times" and "mindful of history" (European history), the two names, Hölderlin and Heidegger, are now
indissolubly linked. They give voice to what is at stake in our era
(*dieser Zeit*). A world age—perhaps the world's old age—is ap-
proaching its end, for we are reaching a completion, closing the
circle of what the philosophical West has called, since Grecian
times and in multiple ways, "knowledge." That is, *technè*. What has
not been deployed, what has been forgotten or rejected in the
midst of this completion—and no doubt from the very beginning—must now clear itself a path to a possible future. Let us agree
to say that this pertains, as Heidegger says himself, to the "task of
thought." Such thought must re-inaugurate history, reopen the
possibility of a world, and pave the way for the improbable, un-
foreseeable advent of a god. Only this might "save" us. For this
task, art (again, *technè*), and in art, poetry, are perhaps able to pro-
vide some signs. At least, that is the hope, fragile, tenuous, and
meager as it is.

While it may not be useful to stress, it is no doubt helpful at
least to remark the following:

1. Such thinking, the thinking of History, is essentially German.
It is not exclusively so, but since the end of the eighteenth century,
Germans have brought it a dimension never attained before or elsewhere; one reason for this, among others, is that the question of
the relation between Modern and Ancient, and of the possibility
of uniqueness or identity for a whole people, has never been so
much a *question* as it has been in Germany. That is, first and foremost, a question for the "nation"—the people—and in the language, a latecomer to the world after the sumptuous, "renascent"
display of European Latinity. German has never ceased aspiring,
on pretense of its strange similarity to Greek (the "language of origin"), to the unique relation it has believed it could establish to
everything most authentically Greek about Greece.

2. Paul Celan (Ancel) was born in Czernowitz, Bukovina, of
German Jewish parents. Whatever the fate of Bukovina in the years
that marked the end of Celan's adolescence (he was born in

1920)—it was, successively, annexed by the U.S.S.R. in 1940, occupied by Germany and Romania in 1941, and reconquered by the Red Army in 1943—Celan was not just at the extreme fringes of *Mitteleuropa*; he was of German birth, born into that language. In a true and understandably forgotten sense, his *nationality* was German. This did not in any way preclude his having a completely different origin, or to be more precise, a completely different heritage. Thus, his language always remained that of the Other, an Other language without an "other language," previously rather than laterally acquired, against which to measure itself. All other languages were necessarily lateral for Celan; he was a great translator.

3. Paul Celan knew, as everything he wrote attests (and first and foremost, his acceptance of German as his working language), that today (*heute*) it is with Germany that we must clarify things.[5] Not only because Celan suffered as the victim of Germany's "Hellenic," "Hyperborean" utopia, but because he knew it was impossible to elude the question that the utopia's atrocity had transformed into an answer, a "solution." He embodied an extreme, eternally insoluble paradox in Germany as one of the few people, almost the only person, to have borne witness to the truth of the question that remains, as ever: (But) who are we (still, today, *heute*)?

4. The extermination gave rise, in its impossible possibility, in its immense and intolerable banality, to the post-Auschwitz era (in Adorno's sense). Celan said: "Death is a master who comes from Germany."[6] It is the impossible possibility, the immense and intolerable banality of our time, of this time (*dieser Zeit*). It is always easy to mock "distress," but we are its contemporaries; we are at the endpoint of what *Nous*, *ratio* and *Logos*, still today (*heute*) the framework for what we are, cannot have failed to show: that murder is the first thing to count on, and elimination the surest means of identification. Today, everywhere, against this black but "enlightened" background, remaining reality is disappearing in the mire of a "globalized" world. Nothing, not even the most obvious phenomena, not even the purest, most wrenching love, can escape this era's shadow: a cancer of the subject, whether in the *ego* or in the masses. To deny this on pretext of avoiding the pull of pathos is

to behave like a sleepwalker. To transform it into pathos, so as to be able "still" to produce art (sentiment, etc.), is unacceptable.

I want to ask the most brutal question possible, at the risk of being obnoxious: Was Celan able to situate not himself, but *us* vis-à-vis "it"? Was poetry still able to? If so, which poetry, and what, in fact, of poetry? Mine is a distant way (distant now by many degrees, heavily layered over the very man who first asked) of repeating Hölderlin's question: *Wozu Dichter?* What for, indeed?

Here is how the two poems I believe carry all the weight of this question have been translated into French:

TÜBINGEN, JANVIER

(André du Bouchet)

A cécité même
mues, pupilles.
Leur—'énigme cela,
qui est pur
jaillissement'—, leur
mémoire de
tours Hölderlin nageant, d'un battement de mouettes
serties.

Visites de menuisiers engloutis par
telles
paroles plongeant:

S'il venait,
venait un homme,
homme venait au monde, aujourd'hui avec
clarté et barbe des
patriarches: il lui faudrait,
dût-il parler de telle
époque, il lui faudrait
babiller uniquement, babiller
toujours et toujours ba-
biller iller.

("Pallaksch. Pallaksch.")

(Martine Broda)

Des yeux sous les paroles
aveuglés.
Leur—"énigme
ce qui naît
de source pur"—, leur
souvenir de
tours Hölderlin nageant, tournoyées
de mouettes.

Visites de menuisiers noyés
à ces
mots qui plongent:

S'il venait,
venait un homme,
venait un homme au monde, aujourd'hui, avec
la barbe de clarté
des patriarches: il devrait,
s'il parlait de ce
temps, il
devrait
bégayer seulement, bégayer
toutoutoujours
bégayer.

("Pallaksch. Pallaksch.")

TODTNAUBERG

(Jean Daive)

Arnika, centaurée, la
boisson du puits avec, au-dessus,
l'astre-dé,

dans le
refuge,

écrite dans le livre
(quel nom portait-il
avant le mien?),

écrite dans ce livre
la ligne,
aujourd'hui, d'une attente:
de qui pense
parole à venir
au coeur,

de la mousse des bois, non aplanie,
orchis et orchis, clairsemé,

de la verdeur, plus tard, en voyage,
distincte,

qui nous conduit, l'homme,
qui, à cela, tend l'oreille,

les chemins
de rondins à demi
parcourus dans la fange,

de l'humide,
très.

(André du Bouchet)

Arnika, luminet, cette
gorgée du puits au
cube étoilé plus haut du dé,

dans la
hutte,

là, dans un livre
—les noms, de qui, relevés
avant le mien?—
là, dans un livre,
lignes qui inscrivent
une attente, aujourd'hui,
de qui méditera (à
venir, in-
cessamment venir)
un mot
du coeur

humus des bois, jamais aplani,

orchis, orchis,
unique,

chose crue, plus tard, chemin faisant,
claire,

qui nous voitura,
l'homme,
lui-même à son écoute,

à moitié
frayé le layon de rondins
là-haut dans le marais,

humide,
oui.

(At the end of André du Bouchet's slim volume, we read the following note: "'Todtnauberg' was translated using the initial version
of the poem, dated 'Frankfurt am Main, 2 August 1967.' From a
word-for-word translation suggested by Paul Celan, I have kept the
French 'qui nous voitura' for 'der uns fährt.' A.d.B.")

I am not juxtaposing these translations here in order to compare
or comment on them. It is not my intention to "critique" them. At
most, I think it necessary to remark that what we might call the
"Mallarmean" style of André du Bouchet's translations, their effete
or precious quality, does not do justice to the lapidary hardness,
the abruptness of language as handled by Celan. Or rather, the language that held him, ran through him. Especially in his late work,
prosody and syntax do violence to language: they chop, dislocate,
truncate or cut it. Something in this certainly bears comparison to
what occurs in Hölderlin's last, "paratactic" efforts, as Adorno calls
them: condensation and juxtaposition, a strangling of language.
But no lexical "refinement," or very little; even when he opts for a
sort of "surreal" handling of metaphor or "image," he does not de-
part from essentially simple, naked language. For example, the
"such" (*telle*) used twice as a demonstrative in the "Mallarmean"

translation of "Tübingen, January" is a turn of phrase totally foreign to Celan's style. Even more so the "A cécité même / mue, pupilles" ("To blindness itself / moved, pupils") that begins the same poem in what is indeed the most obscure way possible. But I do not wish to reopen the polemic initiated a decade or so ago by Meschonnic.[7]

No, though I recall these translations, and though I will even, in turn, try my hand at translating, I do not wish to play at comparison—a game of limited interest. Nor do I cite them as an obligatory preamble to commentary. I give the translations only so we can see where we stand. I believe these poems to be completely untranslatable, including within their own language, and indeed, for this reason, invulnerable to commentary. They *necessarily* escape interpretation; they forbid it. One could even say they are written to forbid it. This is why the sole question carrying them, as it carried all Celan's poetry, is that of meaning, the possibility of meaning. A transcendental question, one might say, which does to some extent inscribe Celan in Hölderlin's lineage or wake: that of "poetry's poetry" (without, of course, the least concession to any sort of "formalism"). And a question that inevitably takes away, as Heidegger found with both Hölderlin and Trakl, all forms of hermeneutic power, even at one remove: for example, envisioning a "hermeneutics of hermeneutics." For in any case, sooner or later one finds oneself back at "wanting to say nothing," which exceeds (or falls short of) all "wanting to say," all intention of signifying, since it is always caught in advance in an archetypal double bind of the "Don't read me" sort; in this instance, something like, "Don't believe in meaning anymore." Since Rimbaud's time, let's say, this has always amounted to saying "Believe *me*, don't believe in meaning anymore," which at once raises and demotes, pathetically, risibly, or fraudulently, the "I" that thus projects itself to (and from) the function of incarnating meaning.

The question I ask myself is indeed that of the subject, that cancer of the subject, both the ego's and the masses'. Because it is first the question of whoever today (*heute*) might speak a language other than the subject's, and attest or respond to the unprecedented ig-

nominy that the "age of the subject" rendered itself—and remains—guilty of. At least since Schlegel and Hegel, it is also, indissociably, the question of the lyric: is lyric a "subjective" genre?
In sum, it is the question of the banished singularity of the subject
or, what amounts to the same thing, the question of idiom, of
"pure idiom," if that can exist. Is it possible, and necessary, to
wrench oneself out of the language of the age? To say what? Or
rather, to speak what?

Such a question, as you perceive—and here I am barely shifting
angles—is no different from that of the relation between "poetry
and thought," *Dichten und Denken,* a question indeed specifically
asked in German. What is a work of poetry that, forswearing the
repetition of the disastrous, deadly, already-said, makes itself absolutely singular? What should we think of poetry (or what of
thought is left in poetry) that must refuse, sometimes with great
stubbornness, to signify? Or, simply, what is a poem whose "cod-
ing" is such that it foils in advance all attempts to decipher it?

I have been asking myself this question, which I grant is naïve,
for a long time, and especially since reading Peter Szondi's analysis
of "Du liegst . . . ,"[8] the poem on Berlin written in 1967 and published in *Schneepart* in 1971; it is, along with two essays by Blanchot
and by Lévinas published in 1972 in the *Revue des belles lettres* ("Le
dernier à parler" and "De l'être à l'autre"[9]), among the very few il-
luminating commentaries on Celan. But whereas Blanchot's and
Lévinas's readings remain "gnomic," to recall Adorno's objection to
Heidegger's interpretation of Hölderlin[10]—that is, they found their
arguments on phrases lifted from Celan's poems (his verse contains
many such isolatable bits, as does all "thinking poetry")—Szondi's
analysis is to my knowledge the only one[11] to completely decipher
a poem, down to its most resistant opacities, because it is the only
one to know what "material" gave rise to the work: the circumstances remembered, the places traveled to, the words exchanged,
the sights glimpsed or contemplated, and so on. Szondi scouts out
the least allusion, the slightest evocation. The result is a translation
in which almost nothing is left over; *almost,* because we must still
explain, beyond Szondi's delight at having been present in the right

place at the right time, a poetry based on the exploitation of such "singularity," and thus (i.e., in this respect) forever inaccessible to those who did not initially witness what the poetry transformed into a very laconic "story" or a very allusive "evocation." The question I have called that of idiom is therefore more exactly that of singularity. We must avoid confusing this with another, relatively secondary or derivative question, that of the "readable" and the "unreadable." My question asks not just about the "text," but about the singular *experience* coming into writing; it asks if, being singular, experience can be written, or if from the moment of writing its very singularity is not forever lost and borne away in one way or another, at origin or en route to destination, by the very fact of language. This could be due to language's impossible intransitivity, or to the desire for meaning, for universality, that animates voices divided by the constraint of a language that is itself, in turn, only one of many. Is there, can there be, a singular experience? A silent experience, absolutely untouched by language, unprompted by even the most slightly articulated discourse? If, impossibly, we can say "yes," if singularity exists or subsists despite all odds (and beyond all empirical considerations, the presence of a witness such as Peter Szondi, for example, or of someone else who knows), can language possibly take on its burden? And would idiom suffice for the purpose—idiom of course different from the facile "crypting" or refusal to reveal one's point so terribly endemic to the "modern"? These questions pose neither the problem of solipsism nor that of autism, but very probably that of solitude, which Celan experienced to what we must justly call the utmost degree.

I reread "Tübingen, January" (a poem with an old-fashioned date, *Jänner* for *Januar*, as if in allusion to Hölderlin's disconcerting manner of dating poems during his "mad" period); I reread it as I read it, as I understand it, as I thus cannot but translate it. This effort is partly unnecessary because of Martine Broda's beautiful French translation, which to my mind can hardly be improved upon, and from which I will at least borrow the unsurpassable phrase "wheeled with gulls" ("tour / noyées de mouettes").[12] But I cannot help translating here. So I return, with emendations, to a rendering I attempted a few years ago while working on Hölderlin:

TÜBINGEN, JANVIER

Sous un flot d'éloquence
aveuglés, les yeux.
Leur—"une
énigme est le
pur jailli"—, leur
mémoire de
tours Hölderlin nageant, tournoyées de mouettes.

Visites de menuisiers submergés sous
ces
paroles plongeant:

Viendrait,
viendrait un homme
viendrait un homme au monde, aujourd'hui, avec
la barbe de lumière des Patriarches: il n'aurait,
parlerait-il de ce
temps, il
n'aurait
qu'à bégayer, bégayer
sans sans
sans cesse.

("Pallaksch. Pallaksch.")

TÜBINGEN, JANUARY

Beneath a flow of eloquence
blinded, the eyes.
Their—"an
enigma is the
pure sprung forth"—, their
memory of

Hölderlin towers swimming,
wheeled with gulls.

Joiners' visits submerged beneath
these
diving words:

If there came
if there came a man
if there came a man into the world today, with
the beard of light of the
Patriarchs; he would need only,
if he spoke of this
time, he would need only
to stutter, stutter
without, without
without cease.

("Pallaksh. Pallaksh.")[13]

What these few, barely phrased phrases say, in their extenuated, infirm discourse, stuttering on the edge of silence or the incomprehensible (gibberish, idiomatic language: "Pallaksh"), is not a "story"; they do not recount anything, and most certainly not a visit to the *Hölderlinturm* in Tübingen. They undoubtedly mean something; a "message," as it were, is delivered. They present, in any case, an intelligible utterance: if a man, a Jewish man—a Sage, a Prophet, or one of the Righteous, "with / the beard of light of / the Patriarchs,"—wanted today to speak forth about the age as Hölderlin did in his time, he would be condemned to stammer, in the manner, let us say, of Beckett's "metaphysical tramps." He would sink into aphasia (or "pure idiom"), as we are told Hölderlin did; in any case, Hölderlin's "madness" came to define the aphasic myth:

MNEMOSYNE (II)

Ein Zeichen sind wir, deutungslos
Schmerzlos sind wir und haben fast
Die Sprache in der Fremde verloren.[14]

> A sign we are, meaningless
> Painless we are and have nearly
> Lost our language in foreign places.

More precisely, we might say that to speak the age, it would be enough for such a man to stammer-stutter; the age belongs to stammering, to stuttering. Or rather, stuttering is the only "language" of the age. The end of meaning—hiccuping, halting.

Yet this message comes second in the poem; it is a little like the "lesson" or the "moral" of a classic fable; its presence makes explicit, within though slightly detached from the poem (see the colon at the end of the second stanza), what the poem says before—what it says *as* a poem. It is a translation. The idiomatic poem contains its own translation, which is a justification of the idiomatic. Or at least, we can formulate it this way; the problem then becomes knowing *what* it explicitly translates.

I propose to call what it translates "experience," provided that we both understand the word in its strict sense—the Latin *ex-periri*, a crossing through danger—and especially that we avoid associating it with what is "lived," the stuff of anecdotes. *Erfahrung*, then, rather than *Erlebnis*.[15] I say "experience" because what the poem "springs forth" from here—the memory of bedazzlement, which is also the pure dizziness of memory—is precisely that which did not take place, did not happen or occur during the singular event that the poem relates to without relating: the visit, after so many others since the joiner Zimmer's time, to the tower on the Neckar where Hölderlin lived without living for the last thirty-six years of his life—half of his life. A visit in memory of that experience, which is also in the non-form of pure non-event.

I shall try to explain. What the poem indicates and shows, what it moves toward, is its source. A poem is always "en route," "underway," as "The Meridian" recalls.[16] The path the poem seeks to open up here is that of its own source. And making its way thus to its own source, it seeks to reach the general source of poetry. It says, then, or tries to say, the "springing forth" of the poem in its possibility, that is, in its "enigma." "An enigma is the pure sprung forth;"[17] so speaks the first verse to the fourth stanza of the hymn "The Rhine," which in a way is the source here. Hölderlin adds: "Even / The song may hardly reveal it." But if the poem says or tries to say the source in this manner, it says it as inaccessible, or in any case unrevealed "even [by] the song," because in place of the source, and in a way which is itself enigmatic, there is dizziness, the instant of blindness or bedazzlement before the sparkling waters of the Neckar, the fragmenting glitter, the image of the visitors swallowed up. Or because there is also the stark reminder that precisely *in this place*, it was revealed to so many visitors that the source (of the poem, the song) had dried up. And that previously it had indeed been an enigma that sprang forth.

Dizziness can come upon one; it does not simply occur. Or rather, in it, nothing occurs. It is the pure suspension of occurrence: a caesura or a syncope. This is what "drawing a blank" means. What is suspended, arrested, tipping suddenly into strangeness, is the presence of the present (the being-present of the present). And what then occurs without occurring (for it is by definition what cannot occur) is—without being—nothingness, the "nothing of being" (*ne-ens*). Dizziness is an *experience* of nothingness, of what is, as Heidegger says, "properly" non-occurrence, nothingness. Nothing in it is "lived," as in all experience, because all experience is the experience of nothingness: the experience of dizziness here, as much as the anguish Heidegger describes, or as much as laughter in Bataille. Or the lightning recognition of love. As much as all the infinitely paradoxical, "impossible" experiences of death, of disappearance in the present. How poignant and difficult to think that Celan chose his own death (the most finite infinite choice), throwing himself into the waters of the Seine.

To say this again in another way: there is no "poetic experience" in the sense of a "lived moment" or a poetic "state." If such a thing exists, or thinks it does—for after all it is the power, or impotence, of literature to believe and make others believe this—it cannot give rise to a poem. To a story, yes, or to discourse, whether in verse or prose. To "literature," perhaps, at least in the sense we understand it today. But not to a poem. A poem has nothing to recount, noth-

ing to say; what it recounts and says is that from which it wrenches
away as a poem. If we speak of "poetic emotion," we must think
of its cognate *émoi*,[18] whose etymology indicates the absence or de-
privation of strength. "A une passante" is not the nostalgic story of
an encounter, but the entreaty that arises from collapse, the pure
echo of such an *émoi*, a song or a prayer. Benjamin hardly dared
say, though he knew perfectly well, that this is perhaps (and I stress
the "perhaps") what Proust did not understand in understanding
Baudelaire, and probably also what the overly nostalgic Baudelaire
sometimes did not understand in understanding himself (though
he did write the prose poems, which redeem all).[19]

But the poem's "wanting-not-to-say" does not *want* not to say.
A poem wants to say; indeed, it is nothing but pure wanting-to-
say. But pure wanting-to-say nothing, nothingness, that against
which and through which there is presence, what is. And because
nothingness is inaccessible to wanting, the poem's wanting collapses as such (a poem is always involuntary, like anguish, love, and
even self-chosen death); then *nothing* lets itself be said, the thing
itself, and lets itself be said in and by the man who goes to it despite himself, receives it as what cannot be received, and submits
to it. He accepts it, trembling that it should refuse; such a strange,
fleeting, elusive "being" as the meaning of what is.

In the end, if there is no such thing as "poetic experience" it is
simply because experience marks the absence of what is "lived."
This is why, strictly speaking, we can talk of a poetic *existence*, as-
suming existence is what at times puts holes in life, rending it to
put us beside ourselves. It is also why, given that existence is furtive
and discontinuous, poems are rare and necessarily brief, even when
they expand to try to stay the loss or deny the evanescence of what
compelled them into being. Further, this is why there is nothing
necessarily grandiose about the poetic, and why it is generally
wrong to confuse poetry with celebration; one can find, in the
most extreme triviality, in insignificance, perhaps even in frivolity
(where Mallarmé occasionally lost himself), pure, never-pure
strangeness: the *gift of nothing* or *present of nothing* comparable to
the little token one describes, saying: "It's nothing." Indeed, it is

never nothing, it is *nothing*; it can as well be pitiable or totally without grandeur, terrifying or overwhelmingly joyous.

We are told that when Hölderlin went "mad," he constantly repeated, "Nothing is happening to me, nothing is happening to me."

The dizziness of existence is what the poem "Tübingen, January" says. It says it inasmuch as it says *itself* as a poem, inasmuch as it says what arose from, or remains of, the non-occurred in the singular event it commemorates. "In-occurrence" is what wrenches the event from its singularity, so that at the height of singularity, singularity itself vanishes and saying suddenly appears—the poem is possible. *Singbarer Rest*: a singable remainder, as Celan says elsewhere.[20]

This is why the poem commemorates. Its experience is an experience of memory. The poem speaks of *Erinnerung*, but also secretly calls upon the *Andenken* of Hölderlin's poem on Bordeaux, and the *Gedächtnis* where Hölderlin found Mnemosyne's resonance. The poem was not born in the moment of the *Hölderlinturm* visit. Properly speaking, it was not born in any moment. Not only because dizziness or bedazzlement by definition never constitutes a moment, but because what brings on the dizziness and recalls the waters of the Neckar is not those waters, but another river: the Hölderlinian river itself. A double meaning here: first the river, or rivers, that Hölderlin sings (the Rhine, the Ister, the source of the Danube, etc.), and then the river of Hölderlin's poetry. Or, as I've said, the "flood of eloquence."

In "Tübingen, January," the eyes are not in fact blinded; no bedazzlement takes place. They are *zur Blindheit überredete*, persuaded to blindness. But to translate *überreden* by "persuade," or "convince," does not convey the full sense of *über* and all it contains as a signifier of overflow. To be *überredet*—I take this on Michel Deutsch's authority—is simply "to be taken in," "run circles around," overwhelmed by a tide of eloquence. Less "taken for a ride" than "submerged," "drowned," or, most accurately, "to be had." The eyes—the eyes that see Hölderlin's tower, the waters of the Neckar, the wheeling gulls—are blinded by a flood of words or eloquence; the eyes are taken in, and the memory of the river poem "The Rhine" recalls and calls forth the memory of the dizziness, the engulfing bedazzlement: that is, as with all "involuntary memory," the memory of "what was neither purposely nor consciously 'lived' by the subject," as Benjamin perfectly demonstrated for Baudelaire using Freud's argument against Bergson.[21] Thus dizziness here indicates the in-occurrence of which memory—and not merely recollection—is the paradoxical restitution. The dizziness is memory because all real memory is vertiginous, offering the very atopia of existence, what takes place without taking place; giving a gift that forces the poem into thanking, into ecstasy. This is why the poem is obliged into thought: "To think and thank," says the Bremen speech, *"denken und danken,* have the same root in our language. If we follow it to *gedenken, eingedenk sein, Andenken* and *Andacht* we enter the semantic fields of memory and devotion."[22]

Thus, "Tübingen, January" does not say any state of the psyche, any lived experience of the subject, any *Erlebnis.* Nor is it—this follows logically—a celebration of Hölderlin (it comes closer to saying how Hölderlin disappoints). It is definitely *not* a "sentimental" poem, whether in Schiller's or the common sense. The poem says "drowning" in Hölderlin's verse. It says it as its "possibility," a possibility infinitely and interminably paradoxical, because it is the possibility of the poem inasmuch as, possible-impossible, it says, if not the pure impossibility, then at least the scant possibility of poetry.

Here, according to standard procedure, I should begin my commentary. But I have said I will refrain—not to reject commentary in and of itself, but because such commentary, which in any case would be impossible to complete, would require far too much in the present context. Among other things, one would have to read "The Rhine," return generally to the Hölderlinian thematics of the river-/demi-god, and ask what links the entirety of such thematics to the possibility of poetry (art), the opening of a sacred space (and the expectation of a god), the appropriation of the own (and the

Mit
dem Griffel seelenhell,
dem Staubfaden himmelswüst,
der Krone rot
vom Purpurwort, das wir sangen
über, o über
dem Dorn.

PSALM

No one moulds us again out of earth and clay,
no one conjures our dust.
No one.

Praised be your name, no one.
For your sake
we shall flower.
Towards
you.

A nothing
we were, are, shall
remain, flowering:
the nothing-, the
no one's rose.

With our pistil soul-bright,
with our stamen heaven-ravaged,
our corolla red
with the crimson word which we sang
over, O over
the thorn.[30]

As one of those who have undergone the trial of *démesure* and risked being engulfed, as one of the heroes and (near) demi-gods of Hesperia, "The Rhine" names Rousseau: the Rousseau of the *Reveries*, we suppose, in a pure poem of contained flooding eloquence, of *written* drowning in enthusiasm. The poem inaugurates modern lyricism.

DER RHEIN

. . . Halbgötter denk'ich jetzt
Und kennen muss ich die Teuern,
Weil oft ihr Leben so
Die sehnende Brust mir beweget.
Wem aber, wie, Rousseau, dir,
Unüberwindlich die Seele
Die starkausdauernde ward,
Und sicherer Sinn
Und süsse Gabe zu hören,
Zu reden so, dass er aus heiliger Fülle
Wie der Weingott, törig göttlich
Und gesetzlos sie die Sprache der Reinesten gibt
Verständlich den Guten, aber mit Recht
Die Achtungslosen mit Blindheit schlägt
Die entweihenden Knechte, wie nenn ich den Fremden?

THE RHINE

. . . Of demigods now I think
And I must know these dear ones
Because often their lives
Move me and fill me with longing.
But he whose soul, like yours,
Rousseau, ever strong and patient,
Became invincible,
Endowed with steadfast purpose
And a sweet gift of hearing,
Of speaking, so that from holy profusion
Like the wine-god foolishly, divinely
And lawlessly he gives it away,
The language of the purest, comprehensible to the good,
But rightly strikes with blindness the irreverent,
The profaning rabble, what shall I call that stranger?[31]

Rousseau, the "Sage," the "noble spirit"—to whose tomb, says one of Hölderlin's earliest poems, "the child hurries . . . seized by a great shiver"—intercedes; he was the first of his era who understood how to grasp a "sign," the sign from Greece, land of Dionysus: the divine('s) sign. It was therefore he who opened up the possibility of poetry, that is, its *prophetic* possibility. The ode entitled "Rousseau" says so thus:

> Und Strahlen aus der schönern Zeit. Es
> Haben die Boten dein Herz gefunden.
>
> Vernommen hast du sie, verstanden die Sprache der
>   Fremdlinge,
>   Gedeutet ihre Seele! Dem Sehnenden war
>   Der Wink genug, und Winke sind
>   Von Alters her die Sprache der Götter.
>
> Und wunderbar, als hätte von Anbeginn
>   Des Menschen Geist das Werden und Wirken all,
>   Des Lebens alte Weise schon erfahren
>
> Kennt er im ersten Zeichen Vollendetes schon,
>   Und fliegt, der kühne Geist, wie Adler den
>   Gewittern, weissagend seinen
>   Kommenden Göttern, voraus.

> The radiance of a better age. The
> Heralds who looked for your heart have found it.
>
> You've heard and comprehended the strangers' tongue,
>   Interpreted their soul! For the yearning man
>   The hint sufficed, because in hints from
>   Time immemorial the gods have spoken.
>
> And marvellous, as though from the very first
>   The human mind had known all that grows and moves,
>   Foreknown life's melody and rhythm,
>
> In seed grains he can measure the full-grown plant;
>   And flies, bold spirit, flies as the eagles do
>   Ahead of thunderstorms, preceding
>   Gods, his own gods, to announce their coming.[32]

Such is eloquence: the "prophetic tone," or what Hölderlin also calls "eccentric enthusiasm," (another name for "sacred pathos"). In the "time of distress" and the "world's night," between, as Hei-

degger says, "the 'no more' of gods who have fled and the 'not yet'
of the god to come," the possibility of poetry, and with it that of a
world, is ecstasy. And risk; one may be bested, may sink or "touch
bottom," as Nietzsche says, "by way of the truth." Since the fifth
"Promenade," whose place in the exact center of the *Reveries* was
determined by Rousseau's death, water has been precisely the
"reverie" of the dizziness that comes, not from the subject's exalta-
tion, as the reductive interpretation of lyricism always maintains,
but from its loss, or rather from the "forgetting of the self." "The
Meridian" again: "Whoever has art before his eyes and on his
mind . . . has forgotten himself. Art produces a distance from the I.
Art demands here a certain distance, a certain path, in a certain
direction."[33]

Here, among all possible examples, are the last two stanzas of
Rimbaud's poem "Mémoire," on nostalgia and desire, which opens
with "L'eau claire; comme le sel des larmes d'enfance, / L'assaut au
soleil des blancheurs des corps de femmes" ("Clear water; like the
salt of childhood tears; / The assault on the sun by the whiteness
of women's bodies"):

> Jouet de cet oeil d'eau morne, je n'y puis prendre,
> ô canot immobile! oh! bras trop courts! ni l'une
> ni l'autre fleur: ni la jaune qui m'importune,
> là; ni la bleue, amie à l'eau couleur de cendre.
>
> Ah! la poudre des saules qu'une aile secoue!
> Les roses des roseaux dès longtemps dévorées!
> Mon canot, toujour fixe; et sa chaîne tirée
> Au fond de cet oeil d'eau sans bords,—à quelle boue?
>
> Toy of this sad eye of water, I cannot pluck,
> O motionless boat! O arms too short, either this
> Or the other flower; neither the yellow one which bothers me
> There, nor the friendly blue one in the ash-colored water.
>
> Ah! dust of the willows shaken by a wing!
> The roses of the reeds devoured long ago!
> My boat still stationary, and its chain caught
> In the bottom of this rimless eye of water—in what mud?[34]

But Celan's dizziness has a completely different meaning, if only because it is dizziness at the sight of the dizziness just described—a dizziness *au second degré*, as it were. But that does not mean it is lesser, or simulated.

Celan, like Oedipus—the blind man, the "poor stranger" in Greece—is *atheos*. This certainly does not mean "atheist"; "Praise be to you, no one" is a true prayer. Oedipus—but Oedipus without the slightest hope of returning to Colonus, of the Eumenides's sacred wood, of a call originating elsewhere, among the bushes or in the earth, to respond to the prayer and grant it. To signal "all is done," the sin (without sin) is expiated, the suffering is drawing to a close, persecution can no longer take place. For Celan, an exile, persecution was without possible remission—and *what* persecution, compared to that of the royal *pharmakos*. It was unforgettable and indelible; Auschwitz, the purely "unthinkable," had ushered in for all time a "time of distress" that no hope of a god could still buttress.

The time of distress is the time—now our history—of what Hölderlin also called pain (both *Schmerz* and *Leiden*), the word that runs through both "In Lovely Blueness" and modern lyricism, from Baudelaire to Trakl and Mandelstam. Pain, which is not exactly suffering, affects and touches man's "heart"; it is what is most intimate in him; the extreme interior where, in his almost absolute singularity (his ab-soluteness), man—and not the subject—is pure waiting-for-an-other; he is hope of a dialogue, of a way out of solitude. I again cite "The Meridian":

> But I think— . . . I think that it has always belonged to the expectations of the poem in precisely this manner to speak in the cause of the strange—no, I can no longer use this word—in precisely this manner to speak *in the cause of an Other*—who knows, perhaps in the cause of a *wholly Other*.
>
> This "who knows," at which I see I have arrived, is the only thing I can add—on my own, here, today—to the old expectations.
>
> Perhaps, I must now say to myself—and at this point I am making use of a well-known term—perhaps it is now possible to conceive a meeting of this "wholly Other" and an "other" which is not far removed, which is very near.

The poem tarries, stops to catch a scent—like a creature when confronted with such thoughts.

No one can say how long the pause in breath—the thought and the stopping to catch the scent—will last. . . .

The poem is alone. It is alone and underway. Whoever writes it must remain in its company.

But doesn't the poem, for precisely that reason, at this point participate in an encounter—*in the mystery of an encounter?*

The poem wants to reach the Other, it needs the Other, it needs a vis à vis. It searches it out and addresses it. . . .

It becomes dialogue—it is often despairing dialogue.[35]

From that place, that solitude—pain—Celan speaks. It is the same solitude and pain that Hölderlin felt in the end, when he had succumbed to the excess of eloquence and been submerged, reduced to silence, by sacred pathos. "Tübingen, January" is a poem to this pain and solitude because it is the poem *of* this pain and *of* this solitude; that of always being thrown back from the dialogue one had thought possible and then, in withdrawal, "huddling," as Heidegger says of Hölderlin, no longer able to speak; stuttering, swallowed up in idiom. Or falling silent. In a world with nothing and *no one* to authorize or even "guarantee" the least dialogue, the slightest relation to another, however or whoever he may be, how to wrench away from aphasia, from silence? The poem, says Celan, once again in "The Meridian," "today . . . shows a strong inclination towards falling silent. . . . It takes its position . . . at the edge of itself; in order to be able to exist, it without interruption calls and fetches itself from its now-no-longer back into its as-always."[36]

The question of poetry's possibility—and Celan never asked another—is the question of the possibility of such a wrenching. The question of the possibility of *going out of the self.* This also means, as "The Meridian" again recalls, going "outside the human," in the sense, for example (but is this still just *one* example?) that the (finite) transcendence of *Dasein* in the experience of nothingness, in ek-sistence, is a going outside the human: "Here we have stepped beyond human nature, gone outwards, and entered a mysterious realm, yet one turned towards that which is human."[37]

It would be an understatement to say Celan had read Heidegger. Celan's poetry goes beyond even an unreserved recognition of Heidegger; I think one can assert that it is, in its entirety, a dialogue with Heidegger's thought. And essentially with the part of this thought that was a dialogue with Hölderlin's poetry. Without Heidegger's commentary on Hölderlin, "Tübingen, January" would have been impossible; such a poem could simply never have been written. And it would certainly remain incomprehensible if one did not detect in it a *response* to this commentary. Indeed, the dizziness on the edge of Hölderlinian pathos is just as much dizziness vis-à-vis its amplification by Heidegger; vis-à-vis the *belief* in which Heidegger persisted, whatever his sense of "sobriety" in other matters. A belief, not only in the possibility that the word Hölderlin "kept in reserve" might still be heard (by Germany, by us), but also, and perhaps especially, in the possibility that the god this word announced or prophesied might come. This, even though Heidegger maintained until the end, up through the last interviews granted to *Der Spiegel*, that it was also necessary to expect, and prepare for, the definitive decline or in-advent of the god. "Praise be to you, no one."

(In the same way, "Psalm" is indecipherable without Heidegger's meditations on nothingness; it is the prayer born of them. It is indecipherable without the pages of *Principle of Reason, Satz vom Grund*, prompted by Leibniz's question: "Why is there something rather than nothing?" These are pages bent on saying the abyss of being or presence: the *Ab-grund* and *Un-grund*, the without-grounds and the non-ground; they recall Angelus Silesius's famous phrase: "The rose is without a why, blooms because it blooms.")[38]

A dialogue like this in no way requires an encounter—an "effective" encounter, as we say. Probably the opposite. The encounter is also that which can prohibit or break off dialogue. Dialogue, in this sense, is fragility itself.

Yet between Celan and Heidegger, an encounter took place. It happened in 1967, probably during the summer. Celan went to visit Heidegger in Todtnauberg, in the Black Forest chalet (*Hütte*) that was his refuge, the place where he wrote. From this meeting— to which I know there were witnesses, direct or indirect—there remains a poem: a second version of which, in conclusion, I invite you to read.

Here is how I hear it:

TODTNAUBERG

Arnica, baume des yeux, la
gorgée à la fontaine avec
le jet d'étoiles au-dessus,

dans le
chalet,

là, dans le livre
—de qui, les noms qu'il portait
avant le mien?—,
dans ce livre
la ligne écrite sur
un espoir, aujourd'hui,
dans le mot
à venir
d'un penseur,
au coeur,

humus des bois, non aplani,
orchis et orchis, épars,

crudité, plus tard, en voiture,
distincte,

qui nous conduit, l'homme,
à son écoute aussi,
à demi
frayées les sentes
de rondins dans la fange,

humidité,
beaucoup.

TODTNAUBERG

Arnica, eye balm, the
draught at the fountain with
the spray of stars above,

in the
hut,

there, in the book
—whose, the names it bore
before mine?—
in that book
the line written about
a hope, today,
in the coming
word
of a thinker,
in the heart,

woodland humus, unlevelled,
orchis and orchis, scattered,

crudeness, later, in the car,
distinct,

he who drives us, the man,
listening too,

half-
cleared the paths
of logs in the mire,

dampness,
much.

My translation is very rough; witness or not, who can know what the allusions refer to? "Todtnauberg" is really barely a poem; a single nominal phrase, choppy, distended and elliptical, unwilling to take shape, it is not the outline but the remainder—the residue—of an aborted narrative. It consists of brief notes or notations, seemingly jotted in haste with a hope for a future poem, comprehensible only to the one who wrote them. It is an extenuated poem, or, to

36 *Two Poems by Paul Celan*

put it better, a *disappointed* one. It is the poem of a disappointment; as such, it is, and it says, the disappointment of poetry.

One could of course supply a gloss, try to decipher or translate. There is no lack of readable allusions. The *Holzwege*, for example; here they are no longer ways through the forest toward a possible clearing, a *Lichtung*, but paths lost in a marsh where the poem itself gets lost (water again, but without a source—not even; dampness— no more about the dizzying Neckar, the "spirit of the river," the bedazzlement-engulfment. Only an uneasiness). Another example: one could pick, or *cast*, as it were, the image of the spray of stars above the man drinking from the fountain, throwing back his head to the sky: dice thrown like the "golden sickle" abandoned by Hugo's "harvester of eternal summer." And this could be a gesture toward Büchner's Lenz, the figure of the poet, of whom "The Meridian" recalls, "Now and then he experienced a sense of uneasiness because he was not able to walk on his head,"[39] only to add, "Whoever walks on his head, ladies and gentlemen, whoever walks on his head has heaven beneath him as an abyss."[40] An echo, perhaps, of Hölderlin's strange proposition: "Man kann auch in die Höhe *fallen*, so wie in die Tiefe ("One can as well *fall* into height as into depth").[41] One could surely go very far in this direction, as in many another.

But that is not what the poem says, if indeed it is still a poem.

What the poem says is, first, a language: words. German, with Greek and Latin woven in. "Common" language: *Augentrost, Waldwasen, Hochmoor*, and so on. "Learned" language: *Arnika, Orchis*. But still simple, ordinary words. The kind of words in another of Celan's few explanatory prose texts, "Conversation in the Mountains" (a sort of tale, halfway between *Lenz* and *Hassidic Tales*, where two Jews discuss language): words like "turk's-cap lily," "corn-salad," and *"dianthus superbus*, the maiden-pink," that bespeak a native relation to nature (or to the earth, as Heidegger would have said):

> So it was quiet, quiet up there in the mountains. But it was not quiet for long, because when a Jew comes along and meets another, silence cannot last, even in the mountains. Because the Jew and nature are strangers to each other, have always been and still are, even today, even here.

So there they are, the cousins. On the left, the turk's-cap lily blooms, blooms wild, blooms like nowhere else. And on the right, corn-salad, and *dianthus superbus*, the maiden-pink, not far off. But they, those cousins, have no eyes, alas. Or, more exactly: they have, even they have eyes, but with a veil hanging in front of them, no not in front, behind them, a moveable veil. No sooner does an image enter than it gets caught in the web. . . .

Poor lily, poor corn-salad. There they stand, the cousins, on a road in the mountains, the stick silent, the stones silent, and the silence no silence at all. No word has come to an end and no phrase, it is nothing but a pause, an empty space between the words, a blank . . . [42]

Once again, a matter of blindness or half-blindness ("they . . . have no eyes, alas"). But because blindness, blinding—we understand now—is *the empty space between the words* (and doubtless also *a blank*): not having the words to say what is. Words are not innate; language is not altogether a mother tongue (or a father tongue—it hardly matters). There is difficulty with it (there is also perhaps a question of *place* in language).

This difficulty—*the* difficulty—is named in the Bremen address when it evokes, as Blanchot says, "the language through which death came upon him, those near to him, and millions of Jews and non-Jews, *an event without answer*" (my emphasis):[43]

Only one thing remained reachable, close and secure amid all losses: language. Yes, language. In spite of everything, it remained secure against loss. But it had to go through its own lack of answers, through terrifying silence, through the thousand darknesses of murderous speech. It went through. It gave me no words for what was happening, but went through it. Went through and could resurface, 'enriched' by it all.

In this language I tried, during those years and the years after, to write poems: in order to speak, to orient myself, to find out where I was, where I was going, to chart my reality.

It meant movement, you see, something happening, being *en route*, an attempt to find a direction.[44]

What "Todtnauberg" speaks about, then, is this: the language in which Auschwitz was pronounced, and which pronounced Auschwitz.

That is why the poem also says, and says simply, the meaning of the encounter with Heidegger—that is, its disappointment. I suspected as much, but I confess that I was told this, by a friend who had it on the best authority.

To Heidegger the thinker—the German thinker—Celan the poet—the Jewish poet—came with a single yet precise entreaty: that the thinker who listened to poetry; the same thinker who had compromised himself, however briefly and even if in the least shameful way, with just what would result in Auschwitz; the thinker who, however abundant his discussion with National Socialism, had observed total silence on Auschwitz, as history will recall; that he say just a single word: a word about pain. From there, perhaps, all might still be possible. Not "life," which is always possible, which remained possible, as we know, even in Auschwitz, but existence, poetry, speech. Language. That is, relation to others.

Could such a word be *wrenched*?

In the summer of 1967 Celan writes in the guestbook of the *Hütte* in Todtnauberg. He no longer knows who signed before him; signatures—proper names, as it happens—matter little. At issue was a word, just a word. He writes—what? A line, or a verse. He asks only for the word, and the word, of course, is not spoken. Nothing; silence; no one. The in-advent of the word ("the event without answer").

I do not know what word Celan could have expected. What word he felt would have had enough force to wrench him from the threat of aphasia and idiom (in-advent of the word), into which this poem, mumbled against the silence, could only sink as if into a bog. What word could suddenly have constituted an *event*.

I do not know. Yet something tells me it is at once the humblest and most difficult word to say, the one that requires, precisely, "a going out of the self." The word that the West, in its pathos of redemption, has never been able to say. The word it remains for us to learn to speak, lest we should sink ourselves. The word *pardon*.

Celan has placed us before this word. A sign?

PART TWO

Remembering Dates

Perhaps one can say that every poem has its
"20th of January"? Perhaps the novelty of poems
that are written today is to be found in precisely
this point: that here the attempt is most clearly
made to remain mindful of such dates.

"The Meridian"

§ 1 Catastrophe

"Tübingen, January": the Patriarchs' beard of light, the stammering. Might it not be, asks A. R., an allusion to Moses?[1]

Not for a moment had I thought of this. But rereading pages devoted as if despite themselves to the oedipal motif of blinding, as I had to today, I became aware that they may indeed secretly have only one object: the interdiction against representation; or rather, they are haunted solely by the unfigurable or unpresentable. They are fundamentally overwhelmed, more or less unwittingly, by the destruction of metaphor or image that seems to draw in Celan's poetry as its final conquest. "Tübingen, January" shatters an image (the reflection); "Todtnauberg," a poem about the disappointment of poetry, no longer contains any image, unless it is—this should be checked, supposing it could be—the "starred die," the "Sternwürfel" of the third stanza. The extenuation, one might say, of the tropic.

"The Meridian," appropriately, provides some explanation of this.

Appropriately, because the title itself, or more precisely, the word, when it makes its appearance in the course of the speech, does not do so without crossing or intersecting, without "encountering" a certain *Witz* on tropes and (the) tropics. On the plural of "*Trope*": "*Tropen*." Virtually the last words are:

Ladies and gentlemen, I find something which offers me some consolation for having traveled the impossible path, this path of the impossible, in your presence. I find something which binds and which, like
the poem, leads to an encounter. I find something, like language, ab-
stract, yet earthly, terrestrial, something circular, which traverses both
poles and returns to itself, thereby—I am happy to report—even
crossing the tropics and tropes. I find . . . a *meridian*.[2]

The "tropic," then. On the "dialogue" that is the poem, a dialogue
with beings but also with things, we can read:

> When we speak with things in this manner we always find ourselves
> faced with the question of their whence and whither: a question which
> "remains open" and "does not come to an end," which points into
> openness, emptiness, freedom—we are outside, at a considerable
> distance.
>   The poem, I believe, also seeks this place.
>   The poem?
>   The poem with its images and tropes?
>   Ladies and gentlemen, what am I really speaking of, when, from *this*
> direction, in *this* direction, with *these* words, I speak of the poem—no,
> of *the* poem?
>   I am speaking of the poem which does not exist!
>   The absolute poem—no, it does not exist, it cannot exist.
>   But each real poem, even the least pretentious, contains this in-
> escapable question, this incredible demand.
>   And what, then, would the images be?
>   That which is perceived and to be perceived one time, one time
> over and over again, and only now and only here. And the poem
> would then be the place where all tropes and metaphors are developed
> *ad absurdum*. (199; 37–38; 78–79)

How should we understand this?
To even begin to see our way clear, we must consider things
from a greater distance.

The poem, Celan had said earlier—this is my point of depar-
ture—the poem is alone: "Das Gedicht ist einsam" (198; 87; 78).

"Alone" is a word that says singularity—or at least, it makes no sense here except in reference to singularity, to the singular experience. "The poem is alone" means a poem is only *effectively* a poem insofar as it is absolutely singular. This is undoubtedly a definition of poetry's essence (which by itself is not at all "poetic"): there is no poetry, poetry does not occur or take place, and is therefore not repeatedly questioned, except as the event of singularity.

In a way, the effort to say this singularity, or at least designate it, underlies the whole "Meridian" speech—and is always on the verge of breaking through. Circumstances dictated that this effort be directed to a debate or discussion, an *Auseinandersetzung* with Büchner.[3]

The locus of the discussion is the question of art. More precisely, the question of art in relation to poetry. Jean Launay circumscribes the issue in these terms:

> Art is a stranger to poetry—that is, at first, at the time to which the poet's mood always returns when he despairs or hopes too much. And then art is poetry's stranger; art is fascinating for poetry. It indicates the possibility of spectacle; it indicates a window; it invites one to jump. This is also why, in art, there is always the hubbub of a carnival, the drumroll preceding an artist's performance, that is, always more or less that "death-defying leap" which, barring a foolish accident, always ends well.
> The artist lands on his feet. That is what makes him an artist.[4]

This is certainly not incorrect, in any case from the point of view of "theme," as Launay says when justifying comparisons of Celan with Kafka and Egon Friedell.[5] But one sees it is also a complete, preorganized response: the question Celan bears with him and tries to articulate, literally out of breath, no longer resonates. Thus Launay does not entirely do justice to the way Celan proceeds, to the road followed, to the difficult (if not completely "impossible") journey; nor to Celan's precise but complex strategy vis-à-vis Büchner. And above all, *dialectically* re-treating the opposition between art and poetry, reducing the strange to the fascinating by means of a genitive and appropriating it as such (art is poetry's stranger), takes into account neither singularity itself, nor poetry as Celan desperately seeks to understand it.

What does "The Meridian" actually say?

Not, exactly, that art is a stranger to poetry, but that yes, poetry is the interruption of art. Something, if you will, that "takes art's breath away" (I am thinking of the motif of *Atemwende*, of turn-of-breath,[6] which makes its first appearance in Celan here). Or, to recall another of Celan's words, the "step" (*Schritt*) outside art; in French one could say, closely following Derrida's reading of Blanchot, *le pas-d'art* or *le pas-"de l'art."*[7] The event of poetry (and as such, poetry *is* event, and there *is* poetry) is thus a "setting free," a *"Freisetzung"* (194; 34; 75). It is a liberation, not in the sense, common in German, of dismissal, but in the sense of deliverance. And, as we shall see, in the sense of free action. This is perhaps, in a phrase I leave to its own ambiguity, art liberation. And very probably, a certain kind of "end of art."

But the idea that poetry occurs in this manner, when art gives way, and that the poem is said to be "itself" when it is "art-less" or "art-free" (196; 35; 76), does not mean merely that for poetry, art is a form of supervision or oppression. Nor even that art is, strictly speaking, the alienation of poetry. Certainly, art is "strange" (*fremd*). One can thus call it "other," but Celan prefers to say that it is elsewhere or distant, that it is *the* distant and *the* elsewhere (195; 35; 75). Yet in reality, art is only so because it is first uncanny, *unheimlich*: strangely familiar, or, in other words, disorienting, unusual, disquieting. Art is even the Disquieting, as such: *das Unheimliche*. Its strangeness or alterity is thus not a pure alterity. Nor is it a "determinate" alterity in the sense that Hegel speaks of "determinate negation." In relation to a "same" or to a "self," to a "near" or to an "own,"[8] art exists in a strangeness which is itself strange, another alterity. The difference it makes differs from itself; it is unassignable. For this reason it is disquieting rather than "fascinating." It could not be fascinating unless it occupied its own place, exercised attraction in a particular direction. But that is just the point: art has no place of its own. Indeed, there is nothing one can call art proper, properly itself. Without a stable identity, present everywhere but always elsewhere (Celan says that "it possesses, aside from its ability to transform, the gift of ubiquity" [190; 31; 71]), it is not "poetry's stranger." Moreover, this is why, if the task or destination of poetry is to liberate itself from art, this task or destination is nearly impossible. One is never done with art.

It is clear Celan's discourse on art has to do with mimesis. This much should be noted. So should the choice of *unheimlich* (or its equivalent: *ungeheuer*), the word used by Hölderlin, then Heidegger, to translate the Greek *deinos* with which Sophocles names the essence of *techne* in *Antigone*. For Heidegger, art and the work of art are equally *unheimlich*. Celan was no doubt fully aware of this—one respect (though certainly not the only one) in which "The Meridian" is a response to Heidegger. Yet I think it would be more enlightening for a reading of the speech (and for the question I am asking) to focus on art in the explicit debate with Büchner.

Thus defined as *unheimlich*, art is indeed, initially, art as Büchner understands it, or rather as he contests it: artifice and the artificial. It is the marionette or puppet Camille Desmoulins denounces in *Dantons Tod*: "You can see the rope hanging down that jerks it, and . . . the joints creak in five-footed iambics at every step"; it is the monkey in *Woyzeck*, dressed in coat and trousers, or the robots in *Leonce und Lena*, announced "in a pompous tone" as "nothing but art and mechanism, nothing but cardboard and watch springs" (188; 30; 69). In this sense, Launay is right to evoke barkers, circuses, and carnivals. But with literature and poetry, with the *Dichtung* that is Büchner's business, art is really also . . . eloquence, once again. Yet this time it is bombast and turgidity: grandiloquence, with its inevitable effects of *déjà-entendu* and a repetitive, wearisome aspect. Art, says Celan, is an old problem ("hardy, longlived . . . that is to say, eternal"), a "problem which allows a mortal, Camille, and a person who can be understood only in the context of his death, Danton, to string words together at great length. It is easy enough to talk about art" (188; 30; 69).

Yet this kind of determination is not enough; it assigns art too easily, appropriates the *Unheimliche* too rapidly (and in an entirely classical mode, with marionettes, robots, and artificial bombast). This is why, for Celan, art remains what Büchner himself opposes to art thus understood. Namely—according to that most ancient, indestructible model—the natural. Creation, as Camille says in his great speech on art: "[The people] forget God himself, they prefer his bad imitators."[9] So art is simply nature once one takes pains to imitate it. That is, once nature presents a spectacle, enters the realm of representation—in short, when it aligns itself with art. Thus the tableau of the two girls in the valley that Lenz evokes when he speaks of art and defines his (or rather Büchner's) poetics: "At times one would like to be the Medusa's head so as to be able to transform such a group into stone, and call out to the people so that they might see" (191–92; 32; 69). Celan comments on these lines in the following terms: "Ladies and gentlemen, please take note: 'One would like to be the Medusa's head,' in order to comprehend that which is natural as that which is natural, by means of art!" (192; 32; 72). And he adds, a little further on, "As you can see, whenever art makes an appearance . . . [the] pompous tone cannot be ignored" (192; 33; 73).

Behind Büchner's Lenz stands Büchner himself. But behind Büchner, there is the historical (literary historical) Lenz, "Reinhold Lenz, the author of the 'Notes on the Theater.'" Behind him, in turn, the Abbé Mercier, with his phrase *Elargissez l'art.* That this was naturalism's *mot d'ordre* and contains "the social and political roots of Büchner's thought" (191; 32; 71), is scarcely important here. But in its most general sense, torn from historical inscription and context, *Elargissez l'art* tells the very secret of art; it indicates art's movement—and the obscure will presiding over this movement, or animating it from within. Art wants to expand itself; it clamors to be expanded. It wants its difference from the things and beings of nature effaced. In a way, that which is art's own, "proper" to art (to the *Unheimliche*), is the tendency to mitigate differentiation, and in so doing invade and contaminate everything. Or mediate everything, according to Lenz-Büchner's dialectical formulation (nature is only nature by means of art). Thus, to "dis-own" everything. Art is, if the word can be risked, generalized, never-ending "estrangement"—the Medusa's head, the robots, the speeches—without end.

When he brings up this theme, Celan knows he is echoing very ancient "rumors" about art. So ancient that they precede even the (Platonic) philosophical designation of *mimesis*, and its execution or appropriation as representation, reproduction, semblance, or simulation. As imitation. And Celan not only acts as an echo, saying he "listens to the noise persistently" (192; 33; 73), but seems to lend it a favorable ear, bringing back, along with the rumors, the old fear and condemnation of the mimetic (which can be, and has been, conjoined with the interdiction against representation). All Heidegger's strength is required—and even that may not suffice—to dissipate the evil aura of the *Unheimliche*, to lift the harmful and demonic to the level of the "daemonic."[10] Not simply to succumb, opposing it—in the end, dialectically—to the *Heimische-Heimliche*, the *Zuhause*, even the *Heimkehr*, to all the figures and values of the own, the familiar, the "at home," the native land, and so on—the way Celan seems to do when, near the end of "The Meridian," he marks the close of the poetic journey as *"Eine Art Heimkehr,"* "A kind of homecoming" (201; 39; 81).[11]

And it is true that for poetry, what Celan opposes or seems to oppose to the *Unheimliche*, to art (at least "at first," as Launay would say), is, under various names, the own—the own-being: the "self" or "I," even the "he" of singularity (he, Lenz, Lenz himself, and not "Büchner's Lenz"), the "person" Celan also curiously calls the "figure" ("*Gestalt*") (194; 34; 74). Or, to use a word which, though borrowed from Büchner, does not lack religious resonance, the "creature" (197; 36; 77). Nevertheless, despite appearances, it is not simply the subject in the metaphysical sense that is at issue. One word condenses all these names: the human, *das Menschliche*. The human, not man. And not the humanity of man. But the human as what allows there to be one man or another—*that* man there, singular—in the here and now, says Celan. The human, then, as the singular essence (a pure oxymoron, philosophically untenable), the singularity of man or of being-man. It is Camille in

The Death of Danton, as Lucile perceives him when he discourses on art and she does not listen to what he says, but hears him, him particularly, for "language is something personal, something perceptible" (189; 31; 70). Or rather, we suspect, it is Lucile herself, "the one who is blind to art" (189; 31; 70) but who still "perceives" (I will return to this word).

The *Unheimliche,* estrangement, is estrangement of the human taken in this sense. It affects existence, undoes its reality. The *Unheimliche,* despite what Celan's formulations imply, does not open up an *other* domain. It takes us "outside the human" (192; 32; 72), but opens up a domain "turned toward that which is human." Existence itself, but "made strange": "the human feels out of place [*unheimlich*]" (192; 32; 72). Life in art or in light of art, life in the preoccupation with art—even more simply, life benumbed and carried off by art, what I would call life in mimesis or representation, is the life in which *one* "forgets oneself" (193; 33; 73). The result is that Lenz gets lost in his speeches (on literature), that Camille and Danton "spout grand phrases" all the way to the scaffold. And that the Revolution is theater. Again, the motif of eloquence. And dramatization.

But in reality, eloquence precedes dramatization and provides a reason for it: theater and theatricalized existence only *are* because there is discourse. Or rather, *discoursing.* This means that the *Unheimliche* is essentially a matter of language. Or that language is the locus of the *Unheimliche,* if indeed such a locus exists. In other words, language is what "estranges" the human. Not because it is the loss or forgetting of the singular, since by definition language embraces generality (this is a frequent refrain, and an old motif derived from so-called philosophies of existence); but because to speak, to let oneself be caught up and swept away by speech, to trust language, or even, perhaps, to be content to borrow it or submit to it, is to "forget oneself." Language is not the *Unheimliche,* though only language contains the possibility of the *Unheimliche.* But the *Unheimliche* appears, or rather, sets in (and no doubt it is always, already there)—something turns in man and displaces the human, something in man even overturns,[12] perhaps, or turns around, expulsing him from the human—along with a certain posture in language: the "artistic" posture, if you will, or the mimetic. That is, the most "natural" posture in language, as long as one thinks or pre-understands language as a mimeme. In the infinite cross-purposes of the "artistic" and the "natural," in linguistic misprision, the *Unheimliche* is, finally, forgetfulness: forgetting who speaks when I speak, which clearly goes with forgetting to whom I speak when I speak, and who listens when I am spoken to. And, always thus prompted, forgetting what is spoken of.

The motif of forgetfulness and turnaround (reversal) indicates here that the *Unheimliche*, because of language, is the catastrophe of the human.[13] And this explains that poetry—what Celan calls poetry or tries to save with the name of poetry, removing and preserving it from art—is, "every time," the interruption of language: Lucile's absurd "Long live the King!" (189; 31; 70) cried out in despair over Camille's death, and above all Lenz's "terrible silence" (193; 35; 76). The silence that fragments Büchner's narrative, stops it (and stops art, including naturalism), but which already enigmatically signaled its presence in a phrase (without grandiloquence) that says the catastrophe's most secret essence: "now and then he experienced a sense of uneasiness because he was not able to walk on his head" (195; 34; 75).

The interruption of language, the suspension of language, the caesura ("counter-rhythmic rupture," said Hölderlin)[14]—that is poetry, then. "[Robbed] . . . of breath and speech," the "turn" of breath, the "turn at the end of inspiration" (195; 33; 76). Poetry occurs where language, contrary to all expectations, gives way. Precisely at inspiration's failing—and this can be understood in at least two senses. Or, even more precisely, at retained expiration, the breath-holding: when speaking (discoursing) is about to continue, and *someone*, suddenly free, forbids what was to be said. When a word occurs in the pure suspension of speech. Poetry is the spasm or syncope of language.[15] Hölderlin called the caesura "the pure word."[16]

Would it seem, then, that poetry is appropriation, of speech, and, indissociably, of the human? Yes, in a sense. And would this mean that poetry is properly speech, because speech attests to the "presence of the human"? Yes, again; this is indeed what Celan says when he comments on Lucile's "Long live the King!" which he calls—not without philosophical and political risk—a "counter-word" (*Gegenwort*):

> After all the words spoken on the platform (the scaffold)—what a word!
>
> It is a counter-word, a word that severs the "wire," that refuses to bow before the "loiterers and parade horses of history." It is an act of freedom. It is a step.
>
> To be sure, it sounds like an expression of allegiance to the ancien régime—and that might not be a coincidence, in view of what I am venturing to say about the subject now, today. But these words— please allow one who also grew up with the writings of Peter Kropotkin and Gustav Landauer expressly to emphasize the point— these words are not a celebration of the monarchy and a past which should be preserved.
>
> They are a tribute to the majesty of the absurd, which bears witness to mankind's here and now.
>
> That, ladies and gentlemen, has no universally recognized name, but it is, I believe . . . poetry. (189–90; 31; 70)

We should not be too quick—let us use Celan's own political clarification as a model—to stress the undeniable philosophical overdetermination of these remarks. This would be failing them, I think. It would almost be committing them an injustice.

What Celan calls Lucile's "counter-word" does not properly oppose anything, not even the speeches delivered beforehand (Camille and Danton's "grand phrases" at the foot of the scaffold). Not even discourse in general. The counter-word approves nothing either: it says nothing in favor of the monarchy, is not a political word—or even an anarchic one. It is "absurd"; it does not mean anything. But this does not make it "neutral," or if so we would have to agree on the meaning of the term. It is a gesture. It is a counter-word only to the extent it is such a gesture and proceeds, as Büchner says, from a "decision": the gesture of dying or decision to die. By shouting "Long live the King!" Lucile kills herself. Here, the word is suicidal; it is, as Hölderlin said of Greek tragic speech, "deadly-factual . . . [it] truly kills."[17] As pure provocation, it signifies (the decision to die), but in a mode other than signification. It signifies without signifying: it is an act, an event (though I would hesitate somewhat to use the word "performative").

Here is the scene:

(A PATROL enters)

A CITIZEN. Who's there?

LUCILE. Long live the King!

CITIZEN. In the name of the Republic.

She is surrounded by the WATCH and led away.[18]

If Lucile's cry—poetry—properly says what is proper to the human, we must understand the proper here as being like the *own* of "own death." In the counter-word, or rather through the "counter" of the counter-word, the possibility of death "resolutely" opens up, as does something like what Heidegger calls, with respect to *Dasein*, its "ownmost possibility." And from that point on exist—these are Celan's words—"fate" and "direction" (188; 30; 69). That is, liberty. Exactly like the sky opening "as an abyss" beneath Lenz.

In effect, then, poetry says existence: the human. It says existence, not because it takes the opposing course to discourse or because it upsets the *unheimlich* turnaround, the catastrophe of language (the catastrophe that is language); poetry is not a catastrophe of catastrophe. But, because it aggravates the catastrophe itself, it is, one might say, its *literalization*.[19] This is what the "figure" of Lenz signifies: existence suddenly "released" at the height of catastrophe, the "mortal's" sudden revelation of himself as the one whose existence rests on the abyss—the bottomlessness—of the heavens.

This is why poetry does not take place outside art, in some elsewhere supposed to be the other of art or of its strangeness. It takes place in the "strange place" itself. And if Celan says of this place that it is "the place where a person [succeeds] in setting himself free, as an—estranged—I" (195; 34; 75), we must not lose sight of the fact, whatever the dialectical cast of such a remark (very close, as it happens, to Hölderlinian formulations), that the I which thus releases and frees itself, which "comes home," which perhaps even hopes to have reached the "occupiable realm,"[20] this I is in the vicinity of death, silence, and insanity. It falls, it frees itself in the void. If there is appropriation, it is, as in Hölderlin, abysmal. One could almost say that it does not take place as such—and that poetry does not occur, unless it is by default as the *pas-d'art* in art's greatest intimacy, in the very difference of art from itself or in the strangeness to self of strangeness. At the unassignable heart of the *Unheimliche*.

This explains why Büchner—the poet, not the poetician—can occasion, can even be the obviously paradoxical opportunity for the attempt to say the essence of poetry, and thus call art into question:

> And I must now ask if the works of Georg Büchner, the poet of all living beings, do not contain a perhaps muted, perhaps only half conscious, but on that account no less radical—or for precisely that reason in the most basic sense a radical—calling-into-question of art? . . . A calling-into-question, to which all contemporary poetry must return if it is to continue posing questions? To rephrase and anticipate myself somewhat: may we proceed from art as something given, something to be taken for granted, as is now often done; should we, in concrete terms, above all—let us say—follow Mallarmé to his logical conclusion? (192–93; 30; 73)

This also explains, but in reverse, why Celan, faced with what is "so difficult" (200; 38; 80)—not to say impossible—to distinguish (in the last pages he speaks of the "impossible path," the "path of the impossible"), is forced to use a double language. Now the language of simple opposition, which is—though ironically—the language of hope (poetry understood as freeing art, being the end of art):

> Perhaps . . . perhaps poetry, in the company of the I which has forgotten itself, travels the same path as art, toward that which is mysterious [*unheimlich*] and alien [*fremd*]. And once again—but where? but in what place? but how? but as what?—it sets itself free?
>
> In that case art would be the path travelled by poetry—nothing more and nothing less. (193–94; 33–34; 74)

Now, in the midst of difficulty, the language of the impossible: the language of difference, which is not, ironically, the language of despair (poetry understood as the liberation of art; art never done with):

> Poetry: it can signify a turn-of-breath. Who knows, perhaps poetry travels its path—which is also the path of art—for the sake of such a breath turning? Perhaps it succeeds, since strangeness [*das Fremde*], that is, the abyss *and* the Medusa's head, the abyss *and* the robots, seem to lie in the same direction—perhaps it succeeds here in distinguishing between strangeness and strangeness, perhaps at precisely this point the Medusa's head shrivels, perhaps the robots cease to function—for this unique, fleeting moment? Is perhaps at this point, along with the I—with the estranged I, set free *at this point* and *in a similar manner*—is perhaps at this point an Other set free?
>
> Perhaps the poem assumes its own identity as a result . . . and is accordingly able to travel other paths, that is, the paths of art, again and again—in this art-less, art-free manner?
>
> Perhaps. (195–6; 35; 76)

Or yet, and this time in the most demanding, that is to say, the most desperate fashion possible (but always with suitable irony):

> Ladies and gentlemen, I have reached the conclusion—I have returned to the beginning.
>
> *Elargissez l'Art!* This question comes to us with its mysteries [*Unheimlichkeit*], new and old. I approached Büchner in its company—I believed I would once again find it there.
>
> I also had an answer ready, a "Lucilean" counter-word; I wanted to establish something in opposition, I wanted to be there with my contradiction.
>
> Expand art?
>
> No. But accompany art into your own unique place of no escape. And set yourself free.
>
> Here, too, in your presence, I have travelled this path. It was a circle.
>
> Art—and one must also include the Medusa's head, mechanization, robots; the mysterious, indistinguishable, and in the end perhaps the only strangeness [*nur eine Fremde*]—art lives on. (200; 38; 79–80)

If the difference can ever be made, if there exists the slightest possibility of a separation of poetry, then we must think of this difference and this separation as internal to art itself. Inside art, poetry would succeed—perhaps—in withdrawing from art; it would exit art within art. Thus we must think, in art's greatest intimacy and as this intimacy itself, of a sort of spacing or hiatus. A secret gaping. Perhaps intimacy—the "heart" of the same—is always such a gaping, as the possibility for the same to be itself and to join within itself to itself; the pure—empty—articulation of the same. And perhaps for art (the *Unheimliche*), this intimate gaping would be precisely what ceaselessly "estranges" the strangeness of art (of the strange): precisely the caesura of art, the spasm—furtive, hardly felt—of the strange. In which case poetry would not be, in art-outside-of-art, the flaw or failing of art, of language: let us say, silence. But rather the pain of art (of language). Hence the aggravation of the catastrophe, which is, strictly speaking, a revolt (Lucile, Lenz).

This is why poetry, if it ever occurs, occurs as the brutal revelation of the abyss that contains art (language) and nevertheless constitutes it, as such, in its strangeness. Poetry takes place, can take place, in art. But this place is not anyplace. The place of poetry, the place where poetry takes place, every time, is the place without place of the intimate gaping—something we must certainly conceive of as the pure spacing which places (do not) sup-pose and which upholds them, with no hold.

No doubt this is what Celan rigorously calls u-topia:

> Topos study?
> Certainly! But in light of that which is to be studied: in light of u-topia.
> And human beings? And all living creatures?
> In this light. (199; 38; 79)

Poetry, by this account, can be called the abyss of art (language): it makes art (language) abysmal. In all senses. This mode of occurrence, advent, is "proper" to it.

But it does not occur, if ever it does occur, as Poetry, even if afterward it can with difficulty be recognized as such. "The absolute poem—no, it does not exist, it cannot exist" (199; 38; 79). It occurs, then, every time, in the time or betweentime of the caesura, in a syncope, as a poem, that is to say as a word—singular, unique. It occurs in "this unique, fleeting moment" (196; 35; 76), in the "instant" (*Augenblick*), the wink of an eye or the head's inclination (Celan speaks of "the angle of inclination of . . . existence" [197; 36; 77]), in the blink of "release," of the "free act": in the instant of the catastrophe, the revolt—the conversion of the I that opens to existence and allows the human to take "place" within it.

This instant makes a date each time—it is date-making. The poem remains mindful of dates:

> Perhaps one can say that every poem has its "20th of January"? Perhaps the novelty of poems that are written today is to be found in precisely this point that here the attempt is most clearly made to remain mindful of such dates?
>
> But are we all not descended from such dates? And to which dates do we attribute ourselves? (196; 35; 76)

In a way that differs altogether from the standard expression, and thus in its strongest sense, poetry is *occasional poetry*.[21] It is on this account that it keeps, if you will, a dates register, or that it is the search, poem after poem, for the dates an I can ascribe to itself (Celan plays on *schreiben*, "to write," and *zuschreiben*, whose primary meaning is "to note on an account"). It is thus the memory of events, that is, each time, of the singular though certainly not unique advent into existence. Yet this memory is not pure. Likewise, there are probably neither pure events nor pure advents: they are numerous, repeatable, prompted in advance by language. Thus the singular, unique word is, precisely, not unique: the *poem* is always already carried away in the *poems*, which is to say in the infinite approximation of existence that is art, and language. Whatever task or absolute vocation it assigns or accords itself as regards existence (the human), poetry is language. It speaks: "But the poem," says Celan, "does speak! It remains mindful of its dates, but—it speaks" (196; 35; 76). Poetry is thus the memory of dates just strictly insofar as it is *mnemotechne*: an art, after all—of memory. And thus, an art, after all—of language: *logotechne*.

Certainly—we must not be afraid of always having to travel the same circle—memory here is, irreducibly, the memory of a single person. As soon as it speaks and must speak (for this is also its imperative, the "you must" that commands it), the poem can do so only in "its own, its own, individual cause": *in seiner eigenen, alle-reigensten Sache*, in what properly concerns it (196; 35; 76). This is why, at the limit of its own possibility, "at the edge of itself," wrenching itself from its "now-no-longer," toward its "as-always" (197; 36; 77), the poem must clear a way between silence and discourse, between mutism's *saying nothing* and the *saying too much* of eloquence. It is the poem's narrow path, the *straitening*: the path that is "most narrowly" that of the I (200; 38; 80). But this path does not lead to speech or language. It leads to only *one word*, to a "language become reality, language set free under the sign of an individuation which is radical" (197–98; 36; 77). Irreducibly, to the language of a single person: "Then the poem would be—even more clearly than before—the language of an individual which has taken on form; and, in keeping with its innermost nature [*seinem innersten Wesen*] it would also be the present, the here and now" (197–98; 36; 77).

Such is, in sum, the "solitude" of the poem, and what obliges it, with as rigorous an obligation as the obligation to speak, not to "invent" a singular language or build an idiolect from start to finish, but to undo language (semantically and syntactically); disarticulate and rarefy it; cut it up according to a prosody which is neither that of spoken language nor that of earlier poetry; to condense it until one comes to the hard center, the muted resistance where one recognizes a voice that is singular, that is to say, separated from language, as is a tone or a style.

Here, clearly, resides what I have called, for lack of a more judicious term, the "idiomatic" threat: the threat of hermeticism and obscurity. Celan has, if I may put it thus, a very clear awareness of this. He even demands the risk. What is surprising, though, is not that he demands it. The surprise is that this demand is in fact, once again, absolutely paradoxical; for if it is indeed made, as one might expect, in the name of catastrophe itself (in the name of abysmal conversion, or even revolt), that is, in the name of existence, it is rightfully justified or authorized by only one thing: the hope of what Celan calls the "encounter," *die Begegnung* (198; 37; 78).

Just after evoking the one who "walks on his head," and the abyss of the heavens beneath him, Celan says, without ado:

> Ladies and gentlemen, nowadays it is fashionable to reproach poetry with its "obscurity." Permit me now, abruptly—but has not something suddenly appeared on the horizon?—permit me now to quote a maxim by Pascal, a maxim that I read some time ago in Leo Schostow: *Ne nous reprochez pas le manque de clarté puisque nous en faisons profession!* That is, I believe, if not the inherent obscurity of poetry, the obscurity attributed to it for the sake of an encounter—from a great distance or sense of strangeness possibly of its own making. (195; 35; 75)

Obscurity is thus not at all native to poetry; it does not belong to its essence. But it comes upon poetry; it is or can be conjoined with it. That it can thus come upon poetry is precisely only, Celan says, "for the sake of" (*um . . . willen*) the encounter, in the name of and for the love of an encounter, which itself befalls "from a great distance or a sense of strangeness." The paradox here is that obscurity originates in taking the encounter into consideration, and not in the demand for solitude. Celan does not say obscurity is destined to prepare or provoke the encounter, that it is a call to the encounter, or that the encounter is its final aim. He says obscurity is, on the contrary, a mark of attention—even respect—with regard to the encounter. This means the encounter is the occasion, or rather the very *circumstance* of the poem: only once there is an encounter is there the poem's "solitude," and thus obscurity. And in fact:

> The poem is alone. It is alone and underway. Whoever writes it must remain in its company.
> But does not the poem, for precisely that reason, at this point participate in the encounter—*in the mystery of an encounter*? (198; 37; 78)

It is difficult to conceive the encounter, its secret or mystery (*Geheimnis*: a word in which the *Heim* of the near and the own, of the familiar and intimate, still resonates).

In what is perhaps the most striking twist of "The Meridian" (the moment when Celan recognizes that, after all, the poem "does speak," even if "in its own . . . individual cause"), the *other*, indeed, the *wholly other*, abruptly appears to replace the elsewhere and the alien, which until this point had been the only terms in question. It is here that the encounter is decided in its essence and possibility:

> But I think—and this thought can scarcely come as a surprise to you—I think that it has always belonged to the expectations of the poem in precisely this manner to speak in the cause of the strange— no, I can no longer use this word—in precisely this manner—to speak *in the cause of an Other*—who knows, perhaps in the cause of a *wholly Other*.
>
> This "who knows," at which I see I have arrived, is the only thing I can add—on my own, here, today—to the old expectations.
>
> Perhaps, I must now say to myself—and at this point I am making use of a well-known term—perhaps it is now possible to conceive a meeting of this "wholly Other" and an "other" which is not far removed, which is very near. The poem tarries, stops to catch a scent— like a creature when confronted with such thoughts. (196–97; 35–36; 76–77)

This is not, contrary to what one might think, a "forced passage." At most, on the "path" that never stops closing off, coming to nothing or leading back to the same point, it is an attempt at a new clearing. We already know that at any rate there will be no "passage" in "The Meridian."

Nor is this a simple "profession of faith"; the "who knows," which is itself *dated* ("at which I see I have now arrived"), suspends what precedes it. In any case it leaves open the question of existence, or of the possibility of the "wholly other" thus designated. Moreover, the justification for recourse to such an expression is itself particularly discreet and reserved; there is not a word too many, and nothing to flatter the "old expectations" too much.

Yet this said, how is the encounter decided in the substitution of alterity for strangeness? And how is such a substitution possible?

The logic we have already seen at work is still the same: catastrophic and paradoxical. Speaking in its own name or its own individual cause, speaking the language of singularity, of "an individuation which is radical," the poem hopes, has always hoped, precisely in this manner, in *this* language (though it is so difficult to reach), to speak "in the cause of the strange," in the name of the strange and the alien. That is, to use, in and as one's own, proper language, the alien language, the language of estrangement. Celan's brutal reversal here of the movement which up to this point has straitened his gait is simply the sign that between proper and not-proper, near and far, familiar and strange, the exchange is always reversible, and for this reason never stops; it is not fixed and has no determined direction. At the very heart of estrangement or dis-appropriation, by way of an enigmatic trope or turn, appropriation occurs. But this also means that such an appropriation takes place "outside the self." The appropriation, the singular appropriation, is not the appropriation of the self within itself. The self—or the singular I—reaches itself within itself only "outside." Reapplying one of Heidegger's formulas, we can say that the "outside self" is the self's origin. It is thus, for example, that in the last poem of *Die Niemandsrose*, "In der Luft" ("In the Air"), "die Entzweiten" (the disunited) are described: "heimgekehrt in / den unheimlichen Bannstrahl / der die Verstreuten versammelt" ("returned home into / the un-homely banishment / which gathers up the scattered ones" [*GW* i: 290]).[22]

And in fact, the volte or revolt of appropriation does not take *place*. The "here and now" of singular existence is immediately an elsewhere and another time (a date whose memory must be kept). If appropriation occurs, we know it is in u-topia itself. This is why we must substitute for the topological division of here and strange, near and far—which inevitably assigns places—the unlocatable division of difference or alterity. In the place (without place) of the elsewhere, an "other" occurs, that is, a singular existent in whose name—and this time, the expression is apt—the poem maintains the hope of speaking. Estrangement yields ground to the encounter.

But the encounter is no less abysmal than estrangement. As soon as other occurs, as such, there is the threat of an absolute alterity: ab-solute, which forbids or renders impossible all relation. The other, if it is indeed other, is immediately the wholly other. But at the same time, the other, even if wholly other, is, insofar as it is other, unthinkable without relation to the same: as soon as other appears, detaching itself from the same, the same, in advance, has already recovered it and brought it back. It is impossible to think a total unbinding.

Alterity is contradictory in its essence. From precisely this paradox, Western onto-theology up to Hegel and beyond—one might as well say, all our thought—has developed. Here it underpins Celan's entire discourse. But with a very particular accent, once again close to Heidegger's, which aims to remove it from all structuring of a dialectical type, to suspend in it the movement of resolution, to maintain it as pure paradox.

For the same, in turn, is itself only in relation to the other; the beginning of *Die Wissenschaft der Logik* says in substance that the simple and immediate position of the same (of Being) is pure nothingness or empty nothingness. Between the same and the other there is necessarily a relation, a reciprocal relation, or rather, as Hölderlin said, an exchange. One could say that this double relation, which simultaneously divides the same and the other to put them, chiasmatically, in relation to other than what they are, stems *equally* from the sameness of the same and the alterity of the other. But this is not at all so. In the "relating to," it is by definition the movement of alteration that predominates. Or if one prefers, difference is always more primitive. So that in the relation of the same and the other there is an imbalance. This means that it is the alterity of the other, the being-wholly-other of the other or a certain "duplicity" in the other that institutes the same as a relation to the other, and thus always differentiates it. The same is Heraclitus's "one differentiated in itself"—a phrase moreover "rediscovered" by Hölderlin at the dawn of speculative idealism.[23] This is why the wholly other—whether or not the word, for Celan, designates God—de-parts the other, that is, approaches it: re-lates it to the same, which receives it in, or rather *as* its most intimate difference. The wholly other is the gift of the other as the possibility of the same, that is, as the possibility for the same of establishing itself as "differance" (I use Derrida's spelling here for what it indicates as to temporality and the origin of time). The same (the Subject) does not, as speculative logic believes, go outside the self and pass into its other, with a view to turning and relating back to the self so as to establish itself as such. But under the (original) gift of the other to which it already always relates itself, the same is the pure movement that allows the intimate gaping—which is, within the self, its "original outside self" (time)—to hollow itself out, to open and spread.

I may be wrong, but in the first part of *Die Niemandsrose* there are two poems, "Dein Hinübersein" ("Your Being Beyond") and "Zu beiden Händen" ("On Either Hand")—they in fact appear one right after the other—that seem to me to speak not *of* this (they in no way say this very thing), but *from* this. In the first, one reads:

> Gott, das lasen wir, ist
> ein Teil und ein zweiter, zerstreuter:
> im Tod
> all der Gemähten
> wächst er sich zu:
>
> Dorthin
> führt uns der Blick,
> mit dieser
> Hälfte
> haben wir Umgang.
>
> God, so we read, is
> a part and a second, a scattered one:
> in the death
> of all those mown down
> he grows himself whole.

There
our looking leads us,
with this
half
we keep up relations.[24]

And in the second:

> . . . ich
> finde hinaus.
>
> O diese wandernde leere
> gastliche Mitte. Getrennt,
> fall ich dir zu, fällst
> du mir zu, einander
> entfallen, sehn wir
> hindurch:
>
> Das
> Selbe
> hat uns
> verloren, das
> Selbe
> hat uns
> vergessen, das
>
> Selbe
> hat uns—
>
> . . . I
> find my way out.
>
> O this wandering empty
> hospitable midst. Apart,
> I fall to you, you
> fall to me, fallen away
> from each other, we see
> through:
>
> One
> and the same
> has
> lost us, one

> and the same
> has
> forgotten us, one
> and the same
> has—[25]

The substitution of the other and the wholly other for the strange and the elsewhere thus produces an extreme thought of difference. And this thought in turn permits one to think of singularity as the secret—we could also say the intimacy—of the encounter. What Celan calls the encounter is thus first the hollowing out, the intimate gaping of singularity. The encounter is the original intimate ecstasy according to which singular being exists. This is why one can say of the poem which is "alone" that it also takes place "in the mystery of an encounter." It is also why Celan can say the following when he evokes near the end of "The Meridian" the two texts in which he "started to write from a '20th of January'"—the "catastrophic" quatrain I have already cited ("come on your hands to us") and the "Gespräch im Gebirg" ("Conversation in the Mountains"): "In each instance I started to write from a '20th of January,' from my '20th of January.' I encountered . . . myself" (201; 39; 81).

It is true that in the encounter (*Begegnung*), the value of "against" (*gegen*) of "across from" or "vis-à-vis," seems to predominate. A value of opposition. This certainly seems to be the way Celan understands it when he defines the poetic act as "attention," "perception," and "dialogue":

> The poem wants to reach the Other, it needs this Other, it needs a vis-à-vis. It searches it out and addresses it.
>
> Each thing, each person is a form of the Other for the poem, as it makes for this Other.
>
> The poem attempts to pay careful attention to everything it encounters: it has a finer sense of detail, of outline, of structure, of color, and also of the "movements" and the "suggestions." These are, I believe, not qualities gained by an eye competing (or cooperating) with mechanical devices which are continually being brought to a higher degree of perfection. No, it is a concentration which remains aware of all of our dates. . . .

The poem becomes—and under what conditions!—a poem of one who—as before—perceives, who faces that which appears. Who questions this appearing and addresses it. It becomes dialogue—it is often despairing dialogue. (198; 37; 78)

But at the same time, the value of opposition is clearly not the determining value here. It is inevitably attached to the motif of alterity. Yet nothing indicates that it constitutes the concept.

What these lines really seek to say is the poetic act as an act of thought. It is no accident that Celan's definition of attention is, via Benjamin, that of Malebranche: "'Attention'—permit me at this point to quote a maxim of Malebranche which occurs in Walter Benjamin's essay on Kafka: 'Attention is the natural prayer of the soul'" (198; 37; 78). Again, it is no accident that the encounter is defined as a "perceiving" and a "questioning." The "perceiving" (*wahrnehmen*)—and once more we must consider Heidegger, who here, as it happens, is both very far from and near to Benjamin—is the Greek *noein*, thought, the very essence of reason (*Vernunft*); as for the questioning—but here, the proximity is very strange—we well know that Heidegger, in a famous text, said it was nothing less than the "Frommigkeit des Denkens."[26]

Yet thought supposes what I am calling, of course for lack of a better term, intimacy or the intimate difference. It supposes, or more precisely, it originates in intimacy as the possibility of *relating to* in general. It is in this sense that the poem thinks or is a dialogue. The dialogue is a speaking and a naming (which one would have to call "pure" if echoing Benjamin, "essential" if thinking of Heidegger). But speaking and naming are, in turn, a "letting speak." To speak to the other being or thing—to address him or it, is to let what speaks in him or it occur, and accept this word in the very heart of the poem (in its "immediacy and proximity") as the gift of the other. It is to prepare, ecstatically, for the "presence" of the other within oneself; to let intimacy open up.

Only in the realm of this dialogue does that which is addressed take form and gather around the I who is addressing and naming it. But the one who has been addressed and who, by virtue of having been named, has, as it were, become a thou, also brings its otherness along into the present, into this present.—In the here and now of the poem it is still possible—the poem itself, after all, has only this one, unique, limited present—only in this immediacy and proximity does it allow the most idiosyncratic quality of the Other, its time, to participate in the dialogue. (198–99; 37; 78)

The "counter" of the encounter or the against is thus not simply the "counter" of opposition. Rather, in the very vis-à-vis that is the encounter, it is what rids itself of opposition. It is the "counter" of proximity, that is, of de-parting. The other de-parts, close against a proximity such that it makes the very space of intimacy which renders possible thought and word, that is, dialogue. For this reason the poem turns, within itself, to the appearing, to what is "in the process of appearing"; it questions the very coming into presence. The poem (the poetic act), in this mode proper to it (dialogue), is the thought of the present's presence, or of the other of what is present: the thought of no-thingness (of Being), that is to say, the thought of time. "Soviel Gestirne" ("So Many Constellations"):

> ... in den Schluchten,
> da, wo's verglühte, stand
> zitzenprachtig die Zeit,
> an der schon empor- und hinab-
> und hinwegwuchs, was
> ist oder war oder sein wird—,
>
> ich weiss,
> ich weiss und du weisst, wir wussten,
> wir wussten nicht, wir
> waren ja da und nicht dort,
> und zuweilen, wenn
> nur das Nichts zwischen uns stand, fanden
> wir ganz zueinander.
>
> ... in chasms,
> and where they had burnt out,
> splendid with teats, stood Time,

on which already grew up
and down and away all that
is or was or will be—,

I know,
I know and you know, we knew,
we did not know, we
were there, after all, and not there
and at times when
only the void stood between us we got
all the way to each other.[27]

Of course, Celan is not saying time itself, but rather, speaking of
the other who is, in every instance, a particular other, *his* time. The
poetic act (the poem) is a singular experience, the dialogue is a singular dialogue. And this is of course what distinguishes poetry
from thought proper, from the exercise of thought, even (and especially) if poetry thinks. But I do not think one can make this an
argument, as Lévinas does a bit hastily, in favor of who knows what
improbable "beyond" of "ontology"; in favor of a pathos (here,
strictly conceived), of the "otherwise than Being."[28] Certainly poetic questioning begins with a singular address: to the other, in fact
envisaged as a "you." But this address to the you is an address to the
alterity of the you—of *this* other; it is the address, obscurely arisen
from intimacy (from the intimate difference), to the being of the
other, which always "is" and can only "be" Being. How could one
speak at all if Being was not involved? There is no "otherwise than
Being," unless, once again, one understands Being as being, and
misses, in the other, precisely its alterity. Poetry's "you-saying," its
naming, is a way of "Being-saying" other than that which properly
belongs to thought, but still a way of "Being-saying." It is possible
that another space opens up from such a naming, or that naming
sheds a different light on the space opened up by any saying. To
express this, Heidegger uses Hölderlin's word: "the holy" (*das Hei-
lige*). But the other space or the space on which a different light is
shed is not "beyond" Being. The experience of the You, the encounter, opens onto nothing other than the experience of Being:

of the no-thing of being—which Celan designates, precisely in Hölderlin's terms (not Rilke's), as "openness," "emptiness," "freedom." I again quote the decisive passage:

> When we speak with things in this manner we always find ourselves faced with the question of their whence and whither [*nach ihrem Woher und Wohin*]: a question which "remains open" and "does not come to an end," which points into openness, emptiness, freedom— we are outside, at a considerable distance.
>
> The poem, I believe, also seeks this place. (199; 37; 78–79)

In other words, poetry's questioning is meta-physical questioning itself, in the sense that it is the repetition of the meta-physical as Heidegger understands it. It questions in the direction of being as "transcendence as such" (*das transcendens schlechthin*).[29] Just such a "transcendent" is sought in the singular thing or being it is incumbent upon poetry—the poem—to perceive (think): it is the "wholly other," the *arche* and the *telos* of the other, and nothing here permits us to simply identify this wholly other with God. That is why Celan can say of poetic questioning, of the demand or pretension (*Anspruch*) in all poems, even the least pretentious (*anspruchsloseste*) that it is at once "inescapable" and "incredible." The question the poem carries is, as Launay correctly translates, "exorbitant" (199; 38; 79).

In this sense, the poetic act is ecstatic. The exorbitant is the pure transcendence of being. It follows that the poem, as a questioning, is turned toward the open, offered up to it. And the open is itself open, after a fashion, to u-topia, to the place without place of the advent. To put it in other terms, the poetic act is catastrophic: an upsetting relation to what is an upset, in being, in the direction of no-thingness (the abyss).

This is just what justifies the idea that poetry is the interruption of art, that is, the interruption of mimesis. Poetic art consists of perceiving, not representing. Representing, at least according to some of the "ancient rumors," can only be said of the already-present. What is "in the process of appearing" cannot be represented, or if so, we must give a completely different meaning to representation. For poetry, representation is organized starting with what one might call ontic comparison (the comparison of the already-present with the already-present), from which arise figures or images, "metaphors and other tropes," all the turns of phrase that allow a certain use of language to be defined as "poetic." Measured against the requirements of questioning toward Being or presence, the ontic comparison, and therefore the "poetic," have to do with what Heidegger denounced as "idols" (*Götzen*) and problematized as "thinking in models" (*Denken in Modellen*).[30] There is nothing to which one can compare Being: Being is, purely and simply, the unrepresentable.

Poetry as Celan understands it is thus in this sense the interruption of the "poetic." At least, it is defined as a battle against idolatry. All "real" poems, all that are effectively poems, seem to aim at nothing other than being the place where the "poetic" collapses and becomes abysmal. The task of poetry seems to be tirelessly undoing the "poetic"; not by "putting an end" to figures and tropes, but by pushing them *ad absurdum*, as Lucile's "Long live the King!" in the sharp light of death suddenly makes absurd the theatricality and grandiloquence of "historic" discourses. In the highly rigorous sense the term has in Heidegger, poetry would thus be the "deconstruction" of the poetic, that is to say, both of what is recognized as such (here there is a closely fought confrontation with the poetic tradition) and of the spontaneous "poeticity" of language (which supposes the strictest possible language work).

Such a task, which amounts to extenuating the "poetic," is perhaps impossible—Celan is the first to say so. Nevertheless, it is what his poetry strives to do. It strives as "poetry of poetry." But it also strives inasmuch as it seeks to reduce the image to pure perception, that is, seeks to empty or hollow out the image. To the question "And what, then, would the images be?" once the poem condenses in "exorbitant" questioning, the response is: "That which is perceived and to be perceived one time, one time over and over again, and only now and only here" (199; 38; 79). Poetry would thus measure itself against the impossibility of a language without images or the impossibility of what Benjamin calls "pure language," that is, the language of names.[31]

Two remarks to close:

1. In its impossible, exhausting combat with art (the motif of panting, babbling, or stammering), what poetry wants to rid itself of is the beautiful. The poem's threat is the beautiful, and all poems are always too beautiful, even Celan's.

The beautiful is obviously closely linked to mimesis. This is particularly visible in Benjamin, who defines the beautiful "as the object of experience in the state of resemblance." He quotes Valéry on this: "Beauty may require the servile imitation of what is indefinable in objects."[32] If one went so far as to say "the servile imitation of that which is *inimitable* in things," one would reach what makes poetry's essence for Celan, that is, what does not destine it for the beautiful—or for mimesis. But at the same time this pure oxymoron, the imitation of the inimitable, marks the impossibility of poetry. This is where Celan locates the tragic.

2. I do not know, finally, if "Tübingen, Jänner" contains the slightest allusion to Moses and the interdiction against representation. All I know is that Hölderlin, more than has been believed and more than Heideggerian commentary leads us to think, evoked the Patriarchs. "Am Quell der Donau" ("At the Source of the Danube"), for example, says this:

> And think of you, O valleys of the Kaukasos,
> Whatever your antiquity, paradises far,
> And your patriarchs and prophets,
>
> O Mother Asia, and your heroes
> Without fear for the signs of the world,
> Heaven and fate upon their shoulders,
> Rooted on mountaintops days on end,
> Were the first to understand
> Speaking to God
> Alone.[33]

Patriarchs and prophets are named here: those who have known an encounter—a dialogue—with God. Celan would perhaps have said: with the wholly other. And perhaps he would have conceived such a dialogue as poetry itself. Perhaps. Another poem from *Die Niemandsrose*, "Bei Wein und Verlorenheit" ("Over Wine and Lostness"), speaks in this direction. It says:

> ich ritt durch den Schnee, hörst du,
> ich ritt Gott in die Ferne—die Nähe, er sang,
> es war
> unser letzter Rift über
> die Menschen-Hürden.

> Sie duckten sich, wenn
> sie uns über sich hörten, sie
> schrieben, sie
> logen unser Gewieher
> um in eine
> ihrer bebilderten Sprachen.

> I rode through the snow, do you hear,
> I rode God into farness—nearness, he sang,
> it was
> our last ride over
> the human hurdles.

> They ducked when
> they heard us above their heads, they
> wrote, they lied
> our whinnying
> into one
> of their be-imaged languages.[34]

§ 2 Prayer

November 10–15, 1983 (Berkeley)

I said of "Psalm," in *Die Niemandsrose*, that it is a "real prayer."
Just what did I mean?

Three things, it seems to me (I had difficulty articulating them
while improvising a response. And even now, what I propose is
hardly better than a sketch).

1. First of all, I meant simply that "Psalm," at least in its second
stanza, is in standard prayer form:

> Gelobt seist du, Niemand.
> Dir zulieb wollen
> wir blühn.
> Dir
> entgegen.
>
> Praised be your name, no one.
> For your sake
> we shall flower.
> Towards
> you.[1]

The standard form of prayer happens to be invocation and address—laudatory address. Unlike what happens in Trakl's famous
poem, for example, the title "Psalm" is not formally denied; this is
indeed a song or a hymn in honor of . . . No one. Moreover, it is

a near quote, through which it becomes clear that No one is named
in place of the biblical God, the God invoked in Hebrew (then
Christian) liturgy. In place of the creator God to whom the first
stanza alludes:

> Niemand knetet uns wieder aus Erde und Lehm,
> niemand bespricht unsern Staub.
> Niemand.

> No one moulds us again out of earth and clay,
> no one conjures our dust.
> No one.

That is why, for the love of such a "God," man (the "we" who
proffers the prayer) sees and designates himself as a creature: the
no one's rose.

One can of course think that the substitution of "No one" for
God, and the transformation of the substantive (the "common
noun") into a proper noun, are ironical—that this is a sort of sar-
casm bordering on blasphemous parody. "No one" has never been
a name, except in the wily *Witz* Ulysses used to escape the Cyclops,
or in Pessoa. But nothing in the tone of the poem indicates such
an irony. Unless, that is, one understands irony as itself the figure
of despair, a despair here absolute:

> Ein Nichts
> waren wir, sind wir, werden
> wir bleiben, blühend . . .

> A nothing
> we were, are, shall
> remain, flowering . . .

Whence a second possible objection: this poem may be an anti-
or counter-prayer, a sort of "negative" prayer; a prayer whose aim is
to show prayer's inanity. But the prayer form, the invocation, does
not show the inanity of the prayer itself. The prayer seems to nul-
lify itself as an address because it nullifies its addressee by presenting, or naming, him as No one. But "No one" only ever means the

absence or non-existence of the addressee, not that there is no addressee. There is no absurdity in such a proposition. It means simply that by *not* invoking *anyone*,[2] the prayer is indeed empty or
vain, but that by invoking No one it remains a prayer. To put it another way, the paradoxical naming of its addressee makes it at once
(formally) possible, and impossible. It is no less a prayer for that,
in its very impossibility; a prayer and, "who knows," perhaps a *real*
prayer. The paradox here is just the one that ceaselessly creates the
tension in Celan's poetry and thought.

2. To substitute No one for God is to reveal in a dazzling way
that "God" is not, or was not, a name. This poem has an apoca-
lyptic quality.

To say that "God" was not a name amounts to saying that
"God," long thought the name of all names, the name of the name,
designated no one to whom to direct an address; it was a word or a
concept signifying that which was "wholly other" than man, but
neither more nor less a name than "man" is (one can address someone by calling out "Man!" but only when one does not know the
person's name, or when, depending on circumstances, one cannot
or will not say it). As Heidegger says, in substance, before such a
(concept of) God, one can neither kneel, nor offer sacrifices, nor
pray. And if people believed they could address God, call him by
the "name" God, this was no less paradoxical than invoking No
one (the divine, on the other hand, is always named and renamed:
Apollo, Jesus, the oblique "Christ." The biblical god is known by
several names, or an unpronounceable, written one).

That God is not a name, that one can be aware of this even
when invoking him *with* this name, can of course also mean that
God has no name, or that God, the name of the name, is beyond
all names. We know at least this minimum of negative theology:
God exceeds through infinite power (i.e., by his infinite presence)
any kind of assigning. Finite language cannot take the measure of
his infinity. That is, the language of here cannot say what is wholly
other. But that is not what Celan's poem—prayer—reveals. The
poem reveals simply that God, because he is God, is "no one."

That God as such does not exist. His "name" means "no one," his "name" is no one's name. If underlying this revelation there is a sort of accusation—which I think there is; I would say, even, a desperate accusation—it is clearly against theology, which is to say against philosophy. Plato did not only "dispose people toward Christianity"; in Plato's language, our language, all that is divine came, irreversibly, to be said (But if an accusation of this sort is indeed present here, it in no way prohibits the strange elation, the liberty, that traverses the poem).

"God does not exist" is not a declaration of atheism. At most, it *would* be only if "God does not exist" meant "God has never existed." "Psalm" suggests nothing of the sort; rather, it intimates that God has revealed himself to be "no one."[3] Indeed, the *wieder* of the first verse, side by side with *kneten*, is striking:

> Niemand knetet uns wieder aus Erde und Lehm.

> No one moulds us again out of earth and clay.

This clearly means that someone did so in the past; someone, a god, the god of creation, molded us out of earth and clay and conjured our dust. Or at least, we humans believed so; we believed that we were creatures and that someone, the god of this creation, comforted us even in death. Thus defined as mortal creatures, it was possible for us to address the god who de-termined our existence in this manner. But once we no longer define ourselves as mortal creatures, it is revealed that no one created us, that we are nothing—or rather that we are "a nothing," (*ein Nichts*), a *ne-ens*[4] in the sense of *ens creatum*—and that the only prayer it is still in our power to proffer, in echo of the old prayer, is a prayer to No one. It is revealed that Revelation has come to an end. Since this end we can say, in prayer, not that God has never existed, but that we humans have never been, and will never be, anything but "nothings."

The possibility of the Revelation is closely linked—and this has always, necessarily been the case—to the question of man, the essence of man. As soon as man in his essence is no-thing, as soon as the being he is can be defined—in recollection of Angelus

Silesius's abysmal rose, the "rose of nothing" or of nothingness (admirable still, like everything that is)—what has been called "God," the *ens summum*, is revealed no longer to exist. And this non-existence is attested to in its becoming anonymous: the word "God" did not name anyone, or in any case no being in the mode of a being,[5] even one of incomparably more than human being—infinite, supreme, and so on.

We still need to know, however, if "to exist" is the same thing as "to be." I mean simply that the question of God depends on the question of man. Yet the question of man or his essence is not "What is man?" but rather, "Who is man?" Heidegger took it in this form from Hölderlin in an attempt to pry it away from Kant—to the detriment of a programmatic philosophical anthropology. The same goes for God; the question "What is God?" will never reach God himself, in his existence or non-existence. If God is man's other, only one question about him is possible. That is: "Who is God?" Moreover, to the question "What is man?" the answer, today, is always already that man is the subject. This indicates simply that man is God, or the converse.

Celan's extraordinary, "exorbitant" effort consists of keeping open the question "Who?" even with respect to God and even if, as Heidegger says, the question ("Who is the God?") is "perhaps . . . too difficult for man, and asked too early." One hears it resonate, I think, in another poem from *Die Niemandsrose* in which, after a fashion, the Alliance is affirmed:

> Es war Erde in ihnen, und
> sie gruben.
>
> Sie gruben und gruben, so ging
> ihr Tag dahin, ihre Nacht. Und sie lobten nicht Gott,
> der, so hörten sie, alles dies wollte,
> der, so hörten sie, alles dies wusste.
>
> Sie gruben und hörten nichts mehr;
> sie wurden nicht weise, erfanden kein Lied,
> erdachten sich keinerlei Sprache.
> Sie gruben.

Es kam eine Stille, es kam auch ein Sturm,
es kamen die Meere alle.
Ich grabe, du gräbst, und es gräbt auch der Wurm,
und das Singende dort sagt: Sie graben.

O einer, o keiner, o niemand, o du:
Wohin gings, da's nirgendhin ging?
O du gräbst und ich grab, und ich grab mich dir zu,
und am Finger erwacht uns der Ring.

There was earth inside them, and
they dug.

They dug and they dug, so their day
went by for them, their night. And they did not praise God,
who, so they heard, wanted all this,
who, so they heard, knew all this.

They dug and heard nothing more;
they did not grow wise, invented no song,
thought up for themselves no language.
They dug.

There came a stillness, and there came a storm,
and all the oceans came.
I dig, you dig, and the worm digs too,
and that singing out there says: They dig.

O one, o none, o no one, o you:
Where did the way lead when it led nowhere?
O you dig and I dig, and I dig towards you,
and on our finger the ring awakes.[6]

Celan's questioning thus considers the possibility that God—through the "name" "God"—has become anonymous. The revelation of God's anonymity is a historical event (like the Revelation itself). It is perhaps the very event, or advent, of history. God's becoming anonymous (as, I think it probable, the Revelation itself) is historicity; that is, the dislocation of the religious. We are very close here to the meaning of Hölderlin's "retreat" and "return-turning away," or to Nietzsche's "God is dead."

Nietzsche's "God is dead" (let us not forget that *we* are the ones who killed him) produces, however, man's extreme self-assumption as a subject—the subject of the Will to Power. This culminates in an entirely necessary way in what I have found it accurate to call "the subject's plunge into insanity":[7] I am God—Dionysus; or, precisely in the loss of the name, I am all names (the names of history). For behind Nietzsche's "God is dead," there is the (speculative) death of the Luthero-Hegelian God; that is, the absolute, unto-death finitization of God, his absolute becoming man. And this is his resurrection as the Absolute, the subject itself. Celan distances himself from both these ideas—if indeed they are two—of the end of the divine.

On the other hand, the "withdrawal" of the divine in Hölderlin, the "categorical turning away" of the god (the Father, who is the "father of time") that draws on the essence of Greek tragedy, is in no way related to any of the figures of God's death. "Retreat" is not death; it is, on the contrary, what preserves the god and separates the human from the divine, what retraces the limit of finitude, for "the immediate, rigorously considered, is impossible for mortals and immortals alike."[8] Which means at least that the immediacy of the god, his pure and simple epiphany, is—as tragedy attests—man's death, or plunge into turmoil. It is the monstrous (*ungeheuer*) coupling in which the god, too, is lost in man's excess, his enthusiasm. Retreat is thus necessary to preserve the god's "holiness," in the same way that the law commands man to endure the god's "flaw"—because only the flaw helps or saves. For the man returned to earth (catastrophized), such "unfaithfulness" is the height of "piety." This supposes that epiphany always be conceived as the initial moment of retreat, or the initial test of finitude: man's finite being is his being *a-theos*. But it also supposes that the divine be subject to the very history its epiphany—or retreat—sets into motion: the gods have turned away from the world; perhaps a god is still to come.

Celan is closer to this idea. Obviously, he cannot deplore the "lack of sacred or holy names." The god he is thinking of is the Jewish god, and he knows with overwhelming certainty where the nostalgia for *muthos*, and the frenzied attempt at remythologization (which Hölderlin escaped, but with which Heidegger compromised himself well beyond 1933's proclamations) led Germany (Europe). Nevertheless, he shared with Hölderlin, in direct descent from the motif of the "time of distress," the hope of a religion to come. Implicitly, at least. Near the end of "The Meridian," we read:

> Ladies and gentlemen, I am approaching the conclusion. . . . I am approaching the conclusion of . . . "Leonce and Lena."
> And here, with the final two words of the drama,[9] I must pay careful attention, lest, like Karl Emil Franzos, the editor of that "First Complete Critical Edition of Georg Büchner's Collected Works and Posthumous Papers," which the Sauerländer Press published in Frankfurt am Main eighty-one years ago—I must pay careful attention, lest, like *my countryman Karl Emil Franzos, whom I have here found again,* I read "coming" for "comfortable," which is now the accepted variant.[10]
> But on second thought: aren't there quotation marks present in "Leonce and Lena," quotation marks with an invisible smile in the direction of the words? And perhaps these are to be understood not as mere punctuation scratches, but rather as rabbit ears, listening in, somewhat timidly, on themselves and the words?

Celan of course chooses "comfortable." But he chooses it with its quotation marks. It is, moreover, "with that as a starting point"— "but also in the light of utopia"—that he attempts, he says, a "topography," searching for Lenz's and Franzos's place of origin; searching for his own. None of these places can be found; instead, one encounters the meridian, that is, the very line that conducts the poem towards the encounter.

So there will have been at least this possibility suspended before us; a way of saying "who knows?" A religion to come. And even if, after *Die Niemandsrose* and then the explicit turning point of *Atemwende*, the reference to God is, as it were, rarefied; even if a poem in *Die Niemandsrose* speaks of the god who "comes not,"[11] Celan will never have said what, in reading him, I am tempted to say (without wanting to put the words in his mouth); namely, that it is all over; God's becoming-anonymous is irreversible. Celan will have maintained the possibility of prayer.

3. I was thinking, too, of this: mightn't it be that a poem which thus maintains the possibility of prayer—at its outer limit, to be sure—is the sign that a link, and perhaps a necessary link, exists between prayer and poetry? That poetry in its essence is prayer, and conversely, that every prayer is a poem?

The second proposition apparently poses little difficulty; after all, the sole archives of the divine are poems, and an address to the god, more than any other kind, requires a conversion in language or an entirely different attitude within it. When, in view of the encounter, Celan dedicates the poem to attention, he does not take lightly Malebranche's definition: attention is "the soul's natural prayer." If the idea of prayer magnetizes the poem's search, it is clearly because advocation is here conceived as the original form of address. And prayer is conceived, in a way, as the element of the poetic. But that amounts to saying that in its essence, poetry is prayer. How to understand this?

" . . . I think that it has always belonged to the expectations of the poem . . . to speak *in the cause of an Other*—who knows, perhaps in the cause of a *wholely Other*;"[12] one cannot long pretend not to know that this phrase from "The Meridian" appeals to God. And that it appeals specifically to God so as to say the original hope, and thus the first aim, of poetry. This amounts to structuring the phrase to God, or assigning it, in its essence, to be the word uttered in God's name, for his cause. And finally, to be prayer.

We must not be too quick to believe, however, that such assignment is simply tantamount to renewing onto-theological confusion. Thus invoking the wholly other is obviously risky. But nowhere in "The Meridian" does one find the slightest proposition that would authorize closing the wholly other down onto Being—being which is, moreover, never designated as such, even if it is strictly conceived as no-thingness (that which is open, empty, free), perhaps beyond what Heidegger's statements on poetry as a "topology of being" suggest.[13] The reference to the wholly other, in its suspensive mode (" . . . who knows, perhaps . . . ") is, on the contrary, a question asked, toward God, to the detriment of onto-theology. It is precisely because the being reveals itself as nothingness, no thing, that the God (someone, *einer*) reveals himself as "not one" or "none" (*keiner*), and from there as "no one" (*Niemand*). A no one whom it is (still) possible to address (you, *du*):

> O einer, o keiner, o Niemand, o du.

The movement from nothingness to you indissociably links the movement of the "encounter" and the movement of God's becoming-anonymous. But one must also understand that it is the God, and he alone, who makes possible the address or appeal. That is, the prayer. A God without a name is needed in order to name, in order to say "you," to invoke, and perhaps thus to save names.

Two poems evoke this movement if one attempts to read them together. The poem "Soviel Gestirne" ("So many constellations"), that I have already quoted in part but whose last stanza I would like to cite again:

> ich weiss,
> ich weiss und du weisst, wir wussten,
> wir wussten nicht, wir
> waren ja da und nicht dort,
> und zuweilen, wenn
> nur das Nichts zwischen uns stand, fanden
> wir ganz zueinander.

> I know,
> I know and you know, we knew,
> we did not know, we
> were there, after all, and not there
> and at times when
> only the void stood between us we got
> all the way to each other.[14]

And the very difficult poem "Radix, Matrix":

Wie man zum Stein spricht, wie
du,
mir vom Abgrund her, von
einer Heimat her Ver-
schwisterte, Zu-
geschleuderte, du,
du mir vorzeiten,
du mir im Nichts einer Nacht,
du in der Aber-Nacht Be-
gegnete, du
Aber-Du—:

Damals, da ich nicht da war,
damals, da du
den Acker abschrittst, allein:

Wer,
wer wars, jenes
Geschlecht, jenes gemordete, jenes
schwarz in den Himmel stehende:
Rute und Hode—?

(Wurzel.
Wurzel Abrahams. Wurzel Jesse. Niemandes
Wurzel—o
unser.)

Ja,
wie man zum Stein spricht, wie
du
mit meinen Händen dorthin
und ins Nichts greifst, so
ist, was hier ist:

auch dieser
Fruchtboden klafft,
dieses
Hinab
ist die eine der wild-
blühenden Kronen.

As one speaks to stone, like
you,
from the chasm, from
a home become a
sister to me, hurled
towards me, you,
you that long ago,
you in the nothingness of a night,
you in the multi-night encountered, you
multi-you—:

At that time, when I was not there,
at that time when you
paced the ploughed field, alone:

Who,
who was it, that
lineage, the murdered, that looms
black into the sky:
rod and bulb—?

(Root.
Abraham's root. Jesse's root. No one's
root—O
ours.)

Yes,
as one speaks to stone, as
you
with my hands grope into there,
and into nothing, such
is what is here:

this fertile
soil too gapes,
this
going down
is one of the
crests growing wild.[15]

Among many other things this at least is disclosed: the poem
melds with the address itself; there exists only a sort of nomina-
tion without a name, a "saying-you." The address here—at least
this is one of the poem's possibilities—is the very gesture of love. It
does not say, it *is*, as such, the "encounter," starting from the abyss
or nothingness. That is, starting from death itself; not only the
death-capability of finitude, but, aggravating or having perma-
nently aggravated this, the historically occurred death, the extermination. Starting from annihilation (behind the motif of nothing or nothingness, that particular nothingness is always present. It
will have imposed a wholly other form of the memorable, the unforgettable; another formulation of the question in general; another partition of the thinkable and the unthinkable. It will have
altered thought). But to address someone else, to love him, is necessarily to address in him the wholly other, in the very recognition
of alterity and always under the threat that the alterity might take
refuge in its ab-soluteness. The "you" is divided, and it is not only
in God that one half closes in on itself. The you is also an "Against
you" or a "Not-you" (*Aber-du*), a name—incidentally, untranslatable—that one finds again in "Zürich, Zum Storchen" ("Zürich,
the Stork Inn"), a poem written in memory of an encounter with
Nelly Sachs:

> Vom Zuviel war die Rede, vom
> Zuwenig. Von Du
> und Aber-Du, von
> der Trübung durch Helles, von
> Jüdischem, von
> deinem Gott.

> Of too much was our talk, of
> too little. Of the You
> and Not-You, of
> how clarity troubles, of
> Jewishness, of
> your God.[16]

Calling the You Not-You says: if I call you, it is the other in you that I call in calling you "you"; it is the wholly other, it is God. It is "no one," which remains your place of origin; you whom I call and can call (and it is indeed love, or probably was). From nothingness, calling the wholly other, even if he is "no one," is the very possibility of address, of "speaking to," of "saying-you"; the possibility of the poem as the possibility of "re-lating to" in general. And it is in this sense that every poem is a prayer.

At least until Celan writes the last poem in *Lichtzwang*:

> Wirk nicht voraus,
> sende nicht aus,
> steh
> herein:
>
> durch gründet vom Nichts,
> ledig allen
> Gebets,
> feinfügig, nach
> der Vor-Schrift,
> unüberholbar,
>
> nehm ich dich auf,
> statt aller
> Ruhe.
>
> Do not work ahead,
> do not send forth,
> stand
> into it, enter:
>
> transfounded by nothingness,
> unburdened of all
> prayer,
> microstructured in heeding
> the pre-script,
> unovertakable,
>
> I make you at home,
> instead of all
> rest.[17]

But it is also true that "unburdened of all prayer" remains a prayer, or the citation of one. As recalled in "Treckschutenzeit" ("Hour of the Barge"), another poem from *Lichtzwang*, it is Meister Eckhart's: "Let us pray to God to keep us free and clear of God." Re-cited by Celan, the prayer is addressed to God for *him* to stop the pain, the pure pain that he is in us and between us. Or even, to stop the agony that he is, the agony of death:

> . . . der Enthöhte, geinnigt,
> spricht unter den Stirnen am Ufer:
>
> Todes quitt, Gottes
> quitt.

> . . . cast from the throne, he turned inwards,
> speaks among brows on the shore:
>
> clear of death, clear
> of God.[18]

One could probably say Eckhart's prayer condenses, to the greatest possible degree, all speculative onto-theology. Bernard Böschenstein interprets Celan's re-use of it thus:

> The poet . . . then utters the words of liberation: clear of death, clear / of God. With these words, men would be freed of their burden; they could consciously achieve double death: God's, and that of death itself. For these deaths are linked. Death in Celan is a modern form of the divine presence. His poems receive from death their center of gravity, their sense and their legibility. As the words' magnet, death is their structuring pole. With the death of death, a turning point is reached that ordains a new *poet's vocation*. The last poem in *Lichtzwang* yields the formula: "transfounded by nothingness, / unburdened of all / prayer."[19] It is incumbent upon the poet to accept this new foundation and not to flee into a distant world.[20]

But we should not necessarily understand it this way, if only because Eckhart's formulation, here truncated, modified or diverted, is removed from the properly dialectical syntax it originally possessed: let us pray to God to keep us clear of God. Thus, Celan's introduction of "clear of death" cannot mean "the death of death," which is really the Hegelian notion of God's death (the resurrection) and thus the correct, speculative way to understand Eckhart's phrase. Rather, Celan's formulation means: Given that we no longer owe anything to death, that we have no debt to it or have already paid it everything (the allusion is clear), we are in effect— and without asking God, "who . . . wanted all that / who . . . knew all that"—clear of God. The citation of the prayer is "unburdened of all prayer." The poem arrives in the prayer's stead and in its place; the poem as it is henceforth uttered by the "deposed" or "fallen," the desublimed (*der Enthöhte,* who no longer inhabits the heights), revealing precisely through this that "there is no longer a God," rather than that "there is no God."

Celan's poetry would then perhaps also be the place where the essence of poetry ceases to be prayer. Or more accurately, where it renounces prayer.

§ 3 Sublime

November 21, 1983 (Berkeley)

In J.-F. L.'s lecture on Barnett Newman, "The Sublime and the Avant-garde," I found a passage on Burke particularly striking. J.-F. L. later gave me a copy of his text:

> However much Kant rejects Burke's thesis as empiricism and physiologism, however much he borrows, on the other hand, Burke's analysis of the contradiction characterizing the sentiment of the sublime, he strips Burke's esthetic of what I think is its greatest value, which is to show that the sublime is provoked by *the threat that nothing will happen anymore.* The beautiful gives positive pleasure. But there is another sort of pleasure, linked to a passion stronger than satisfaction, which is pain and the approach of death. In pain the body affects the soul. But the soul can also affect the body as if it felt pain of external origin, just by means of representations unconsciously associated with painful situations. This wholly spiritual passion is called terror in Burke's lexicon. But terrors are linked to being deprived: deprived of light, terror of darkness; deprived of others, terror of solitude; deprived of language, terror of silence; deprived of objects, terror of the void; deprived of life, terror of death. What terrifies is that the possibility of the phrase "It happens that" does not happen; it ceases to happen.
>
> In order for terror to commingle with pleasure and thus create the sentiment of the sublime, it is also necessary, writes Burke, for the threat that produces terror to be suspended, held at a distance, restrained. This suspense, the lessening of a threat or danger, provokes a sort of pleasure which is certainly not that of positive satisfaction,

but rather of relief. It is still privation, but once removed: the soul is deprived of the threat of being deprived of light, language, life. Burke distinguishes the pleasure of second-degree privation from positive pleasure, christening it "delight."

Here, then, is how the sublime sentiment is analyzed: an imposing, powerful object, threatening to deprive the soul of any "It happens," "astonishes" the soul (at lesser degrees of intensity, the soul is seized with admiration, veneration, respect). The soul is made stupid, immobilized; it seems dead. In distancing this threat, art procures the pleasure of relief, delight. Thanks to art, the soul is restored to the agitation between life and death, and this agitation is its health and its life. The sublime for Burke is no longer a question of elevation (which is the category by which Aristotle distinguished tragedy), it is a question of intensification.

This analysis describes what can be strictly called the *economy* of the sublime: the "threat that nothing will happen anymore" (which creates terror), once suspended, still produces pleasure. The pain, at least, is relieved. But it is art that suspends the threat and, in fact, converts the pain into pleasure (or procures the "masochistic" satisfaction that Freud connects to tragedy and relates to the paradoxical tension constitutive of "preliminary pleasure"). With this in mind, I suddenly understand Celan's muted, obstinate rage against art. At base it is quite similar to Bataille's, strange as that may seem. Was Bataille more radical? I'm not sure; less ironic and playful, more emphatic, and not without—I think it was Barthes who noted this—a certain preciousness, encompassed in his "hatred" of what Celan tries to save: poetry.

But this rage, too, responsible for the grandeur of modern art, its hostility toward the beautiful, its obsession with truth—which, in a world without God, in the absence of a world, gives it all its "metaphysical" tension—this rage, too, is perhaps vain. True, "economy" (of art, of poetry, of the beautiful) is appalling in view of the "reality of the real," that is, death and pain. But here is an old argument that Bataille himself recognized as he sought to throw a wrench into the perfect dialectical machinery: what else can one do with death except "simulate" it? Again, he himself called such simulation "experience" (in a sense not dissimilar to mine), provided that the simulation was pushed to the limit of the possible. He thereby indicated what Celan, too, indicates in his own way: that mimesis is the condition for the possibility of thought. An ancient indication (it appears already in Aristotle's *Poetics*), but one that, unbeknownst to him, Kant can perhaps take credit for having mapped out in all its consequences; Heidegger knew this without wanting to admit it, while Nietzsche had lucidly intuited its truth.

What we must think out is indeed the *It happens that*. But from where do we begin to think if not the starting point of "terror," the threat that "It happens that" will stop happening? In other words, from where can we begin to think, we to whom birth has been "given," if not from the starting point of death? Death, that other gift—or more exactly, the pro-spect of the first and only one (the enigma of our birth is before us). The question torments Celan's poetry. In this sense his poetry is sublime, though there is no question of either "elevation" or "intensification." Celan's sublime could be defined, rather, as the sublime of *destitution*.

Withall, does it produce pleasure? Yes, since pleasure is necessarily linked to mimesis (Aristotle again). Yet pleasure in Celan is of a very particular nature. One could qualify it as the pleasure of thought. In fact, it would probably be more accurate to speak of the *emotion of thought*: a contradictory emotion, owing more to Kant's description than to Burke's, and which is basically comparable to the sort of "syncopated" emotion that tragedy provokes (but it is tragedy, the representation of the tragic contradiction, that provides the model for the sublime). One can say of Celan, as of Hölderlin, that he is a tragic poet; perhaps even the last tragic poet—the last "possible"; and one can mock this, as I have often seen done, because only poetry is at stake. (I've also heard the response to this attitude: "It killed him." But that is not an argument. Or if so, it pleads only in favor of the despair of facing art and the impossibility of interrupting it. The argument I would prefer would be this: one could mock such poetry and its sublimity if it were "earnest" verse, something that still exists in large quantities. But Celan, in a certain, secret way one might call elusive, seems sublime despite himself. We must not deflect onto Celan the pathos of some of his readers. And we must not forget, even in Celan's own pathos—for it is there, despite his lapidary formulation and restricted phrasing—the sort of "Jewish joy" [*Freude*], the light, almost silent laugh, perhaps the counterpart to what saves Hölderlin from wallowing in the tragic: another joy, or rather a serenity, in the seriousness of his thought.)

From Kant and the Kantian theory of the sublime, J.-F. L. retains the concept of "negative presentation" (of the Idea). On the basis of this concept, his formula for the sublime is: presenting that the un-presentable exists.

I am not sure this formula is right, and the way I think Celan deals with the question of the representable and the unrepresentable confirms my uncertainty.

Bluntly put, this formula has two flaws: it separates out the un-presentable (positing its existence somewhere beyond presentation) and in so doing, it substantializes or hypostatizes it. By definition, only the presentable is presented. Therefore the unpresentable, if such a thing exists, cannot present itself. Or if it does, it is like the Jewish God in the Hegelian analysis of sublimity, breaking through presentation itself, annihilating it for its greater (dialectical) glory. We would thus need to think, according to the (onto-theological) outline of negative presentation, that there is presentation, not *of* what is beyond presentaion, but *that* there is something beyond presentation. In which case the presentation would indicate, in what is present or insofar as it *does* present, its beyond.

But this beyond is nothing, it is not *a part of* the unpresentable. At most one can say, naturally enough, that presentation is transferred from the unpresented. But the unpresented does not equal the unpresentable. Here is what happens when presentation attempts to indicate its beyond, or rather the (baseless) base, pure nothingness or pure openness, from which it detaches itself as presentation: in or level with presentation, the difference of the presented from presentation presents itself. Difference does not mean inadequation, as a large part of modern art perhaps inevitably holds, for modern art cultivates what is "not beautiful," that is, the simple opposite of the beautiful according to its classical definition: the adequation of form to content. Nor does it mean the reduction of presentation to the purity inherent in the phrase "There is presentation": the white square of the "minimal" that is the end point of negative theology. But it *does* mean the *disappointment* of presentation, or, more broadly, the disappointment that *the presentable exists.* The baseless base of presentation is indicated in the very difficulty of presentation; it does not "come naturally." It is indicated in a sort of internal differentiation of presentation, or, I venture to say, at the heart of the very fact of presenting; indicated in a manner (for it is indeed a matter of style) of making apparent the nonappearing that underpins or, more exactly, withdraws and encloses itself in the midst of presentation. In a manner of making apparent the hiatus of presentation, of retracing the retreat that it is, of *retreating* it.

Modern art, "sublime" art, the art after "the end of art," shows the pain of presentation; it is, or could be, joy itself—or serenity.

§4 Hagiography

December 7, 1983 (Strasbourg)

I page through the *cahier de L'Herne* volume on Heidegger that
Michel Haar sent me. Gadamer's text—a series of "memories"—
ends in the following way:

> Among the many pilgrims who went up to Todtnauberg, Paul Celan,
> too, paid a visit one day to the thinker; from their encounter, a poem
> was born. Food for thought: a persecuted Jew, a poet who lived not in
> Germany but in Paris, but a German poet nonetheless, risks such a
> visit, not without some anxiety. He must have been greeted by that
> "balm for the eyes" (*Augentrost*) that was the little country property
> (*Anwesen*) with its fountain ("topped by a starred wooden die"), and
> the little man, with his rustic appearance and twinkling gaze. He left
> his name in the chalet's guestbook as many had before him, with a few
> lines attesting to a hope he carried in his heart. He took a walk with
> the thinker in soft mountain pastures, each of the men turned inward,
> in his own isolation, like an isolated flower ("orchis and orchis"). Only
> later, once he had returned home, did he see clearly what had seemed
> too appalling in the words Heidegger murmured while walking; he be-
> gan to understand. He understood the audacity of a thought that an-
> other ("the man") can hear without capturing its meaning, the risk of
> a step that moves forward on shifting terrain, like on the logging paths
> one cannot follow to an end.

Here is the poem:

92

TODTNAUBERG

Arnica, little-light balm,
the elixir of the fountain topped by the
starred wooden die;

in the
chalet,

the lines on the book
—whose, the name named
before mine?—
inscribed in this book
the lines hoping, today,
for the word
to come
from a thinker,
at heart

Sylvan prairies of uneven earth,
orchis and orchis, isolatedly,

Appalling, what later, en route,
became clear
He who guides us, this man
listens to us too,
on the path
of logs

half
covered in mire,

damp,

many.[1]

One could entitle this piece "birth of a hagiography."

My initial anger having passed, Marc B. de Launay's French translation nevertheless holds my attention. It is certainly more "accurate" than all the others, but it explicates the poem strangely, at least on two points. First, the *Sternwürfel* of the third verse:

der
Trunk aus dem Brunnen mit dem
Sternwürfel drauf

is rendered as: "the elixir of the fountain topped by the / starred
wooden die." "Elixir" is clearly a result of Gadamer's edifying fable: "He [Celan] must have been greeted by the 'balm for the eyes'
(*Augentrost*) that was the little country property (*Anwesen*) with its
fountain ('topped by a starred wooden die'), and the little man,
with his rustic appearance and twinkling gaze." Drinking a draught
of water at said fountain seems nearly like imbibing a miraculous
elixir. . . . But the "starred wooden die" is only possible if one is
familiar with the *Anwesen* in question—and if one translates, even
in German, the formation *Sternwürfel.* Such a "translation" is plau-
sible, and eliminates the sole image that this poem without images
might still have contained. It should perhaps be given credit for its
prosaic quality.

The second point concerns the verses:

Krudes, später, in Fahren,
deutlich

which are explicated in the following manner: "Appalling, what
later, en route, / became clear." Marc B. de Launay could not have
translated otherwise; after all, he had to transcribe Gadamer's interpretation. ("Only later, once he had returned home, did he see
clearly what had seemed too appalling in the words Heidegger
murmured while walking; he began to understand.") I have been
told more than once—and not only by D.C.—that Celan had returned from the encounter in a state of despair. The expression
B.B. used was even: "I saw him when he returned to Frankfurt; he
was sick about it." Yes, the birth of a hagiography.

§ 5 The Power of Naming

December 28, 1983 (Les Ayes)

The question implied by the appeal to the wholly other—again I come back to this—is double: it concerns the existence of the wholly other, but also, at the same time, the possibility of speaking in his name (or in his absence-of-name). Inasmuch as it concerns the existence of the wholly other, it implies another, underlying question, perhaps the only question of "The Meridian": is to exist simply to be? To attempt to formulate it once again: it goes without saying that only what is, exists—in the mode of being. But does that really mean that existence consists solely of "being (*être*) in the mode of being (*étant*)"? The question applies first to man, the only creature who, as Rousseau says, "feels his existence." This feeling as Celan's writing allows us to approach it is contained in three "abilities": the ability to die, the ability to receive (relate to), and the ability to think (perceive). These three are united in the ability to speak, through which the fact of presence is generally attested, and also through which man, attesting that he is (present), attests *who* he is: the one who exists as the being capable of attesting presence and absence in general.

Existence would thus be language, or more precisely, the faculty of language, which, in the being (*étant*) that is man, does not come under the heading of being—so that man "is" not only the being that he is. The faculty of language, the ability to name, is in reality

intimacy itself, the intimate differentiation of the being. Through
this differentiation, man, beyond what he is, corresponds to a being (*l'être*) by naming what is, by naming himself, by naming who
he is not (God). For this reason language is not, in its essence,
purely and simply being (*étant*); yet there *is* language, or language
exists—like the possibility of relating to (addressing), which is
closer to our origins than any form of "communication." Language
is the other in man; it constitutes him as man *himself.* Man does
not *have* language in the sense of possession or property; "language
is what is proper to man" means that man is constituted beginning
with language; he is not its master (on the contrary; language op-
erates a strange dispossession, attracting man—within himself—
outside of himself). This is the motif of "pre-scription" (*Vor-Schrift*).
Language is the essence, the inhuman essence, of man; it is his
(in)humanity.

Thus, language can be considered man's origin. Not as God is,
according to the onto-theological structure established in the first
lines of the fourth gospel Ἐυ ἀρχῇ ἦυ ὁ λόγος .But as that by which
man is necessarily related to the other, and thence to the wholly
other, so that God is not language, but its supposition, or at least
what irresistibly draws it. It is perhaps what has been called ψυχή,
anima, the soul, provided these words carry no echo of any substance, that is, of any subject. Intimacy, in its very differ*a*nce, re-
treats from all subjects. It is nothing but the gaping of the subject.
And the gaping is language. Language in the *interior intimo meo*
that onto-theology confused with God.

From that might follow this: when poetry accomplishes its task,
which is to push itself to the origin of language (a task that is by
definition impossible); when it strains to "dig" right to language's
possibility; it encounters, at the edge of the inaccessible and for-
ever-concealed gaping, the naked possibility of address.

And from that would then follow this: if God exists, he exists as
a speaking being, and is thus himself subject to language. The fact
that he is now silent, that he has ceased to speak, perhaps delivers
us from the irresistible magnetization he creates in language; it de-

livers us from prayer. One might then catch sight of a wholly other poetry, which is perhaps what Celan did glimpse in the end, and what made him despair.

§6 Pain

February 7, 1984 (Tübingen)

Perhaps all I've ever done is move back and forth, more or less unwittingly, between two or three passages of Heidegger's *Unterwegs zur Sprache* (*On the Way to Language*), which I recently reread after an abundance of other reading:

> Experience means *eundo assequi*, to obtain something along the way, to attain something by going on a way.[1]

> To undergo an experience with something—be it a thing, a person, or a god—means that this something befalls us, strikes us, comes over us, overwhelms and transforms us. When we talk of "undergoing" an experience, we mean specifically that the experience is not of our own making; to undergo here means that we endure it, suffer it, receive it as it strikes us and submit to it.[2]

> But the more joyful the joy, the more pure the sadness slumbering within it. The deeper the sadness, the more summoning the joy resting within it. Sadness and joy play into each other. The play itself which attunes the two by letting the remote be near and the near be remote is pain. This is why both, highest joy and deepest sadness, are painful each in its way. But pain so touches the spirit of mortals that the spirit receives its gravity from pain. That gravity keeps mortals with all their wavering at rest in their being. The spirit which answers to pain, the spirit attuned by pain and to pain, is melancholy.[3]

> But what is pain? Pain rends. It is the rift. But it does not tear apart

into dispersive fragments. Pain indeed tears asunder, it separates, yet so that at the same time it draws everything to itself, gathers it to itself. Its rending, as a separating that gathers, is at the same time that drawing which, like the pen-drawing of a plan or sketch, draws and joins together what is held apart in separation. Pain is the joining agent in the rending that divides and gathers. Pain is the joining of the rift. . . . Pain joins the rift of the difference. Pain is the dif-ference itself.[4]

In connecting these texts, I think of the passage from the letter to Jünger, *Zur Seinsfrage*, which happens to deal with lines and meridians (Jünger's expression is "the zero meridian," by which he means the boundary of nihilism, considered by Heidegger to be an insurmountable barrier). I think of the passage in which Heidegger, speaking of his work on the negative and its pain in the Hegelian dialectic, suggests that ἄλγος and λόγος have a common root. It hardly matters whether this is true or not. The idea is that a constraint more ancient than philosophy made the height of philosophy "logic," that is, the thought of pain. That Heidegger's ceaseless return to the motif of pain in his readings of Hölderlin, Trakl, George—of poetry—is a sure indication that in his eyes, it is urgent to pry the essence of pain, and thus of language, away from its negative, laborious and servile definition. Or that it is urgent to think of difference as other than negative. Had I been capable of it, I would have shown that in this sense, Celan's poetry is a poetry of pain; I would have shown that that is lyricism.

There is another passage in *Unterwegs zur Sprache*; it concerns solitude (and this one, when I read it, rang no bell, however faint, in my memory):

Only he can be lonesome who is not alone, if "not alone" means not apart, singular, without any rapports. But it is precisely the absence in the lonesome of something in common which persists as the most binding bond *with* it. The "some" in lonesome is the Gothic *sama*, the Greek *hama*, and the English *same*. "Lonesome" means: the same in what unites that which belongs together.[5]

Could this be the starting point for trying to understand the problem of what Celan calls "the encounter"? But to what community could (the poem's) solitude, the lack of community, be related in the most sociable manner? Perhaps the one that incarnates not the lack, but the destruction of all community. Such a designation goes, not exclusively but first, to the Jewish people. *Die Niemandsrose* is dedicated to Osip Mandelstam.

Postscript: a few days later, J. Le R. sends me a translation of "Tübingen, Jänner" by Jean-Pierre Lefebvre. It follows:

> His eyes worn down
> unto blindness by discourse,
> Their—"an enigma is pure
> gushing forth"—, their
> memory of
> Hölderlin towers encircled
> with seagulls' cries.
> His drowned joiners' visits to
> these
> diving words:
>
> If there came,
> if there came a man,
> if a there came a man into the world, today, with
> the beard of light of
> the Patriarchs: he could,
> if he spoke of this
> time, he
> could only mumble, and mumble
> still, mu-mumble all-
> ways, ways.
> ("Pallaksch. Pallaksch.")[6]

Earlier J. Le R. had drawn my attention to the motif of blindness "as lucidity." He cited as support for his claim these verses from *Die Niemandsrose*:

Wer
sagt, dass uns alles erstarb,
da uns das Aug brach?
Alles erwachte, alles hob an.

Who
says that everything died for us
when our eyes broke?
Everything awakened, everything began.[7]

I was reminded of a passage in Blanchot's *Le dernier à parler*
(*The Last to Speak*):

Perhaps the recourse—is it a recourse, an appeal?—is to give oneself over, beyond the language mesh ("Eye's roundness between the
bars.")[8] to waiting for a wider gaze, for the possibility of seeing, of seeing without the very words that signify sight:

Do not read any more—look!
Do not look any more—go![9]

Sight, then (perhaps), but always *in view of* movement, associated
with movement. As if the idea was to go toward the appeal of eyes
that see beyond what there is to see: "eyes world-blind,"[10] "eyes
submerged by words, unto blindness";[11] eyes that look (or have
their place) "in the fissure of dying."[12]

Eyes world-blind,
eyes in the fissure of dying, eyes, eyes . . .
Do not read any more—look!
Do not look any more—go![13]

In Hölderlin, the most lucid blindmen are Tiresias and especially
Oedipus (a surfeit of eyes). It was to this motif I sought to relate
the "eyes submerged by words, unto blindness," as Blanchot translates. The gaze beyond the gaze, the view of beyond-viewing,
would be *spare*. But in "Tübingen, Jänner," the spareness becomes,
in the absence of eloquence, pitiful stammering.

§7 Ecstasy

March 5, 1984 (Strasbourg)

The model for ecstasy in the *Reveries* is the rapture that seizes Rousseau when he regains consciousness after an accident that occurs as he descends the hill from Ménilmontant to Paris ("Second Walk"):

> Night was coming on. I saw the sky, some stars, and a few leaves. This first sensation was a moment of delight. I was conscious of nothing else. In this instant I was being born again, and it seemed as if all I perceived was filled with my frail existence. Entirely taken up by the present, I could remember nothing; I had no distinct notion of myself as a person, nor had I the least idea of what had just happened to me. I did not know who I was, nor where I was; I felt neither pain, fear, nor anxiety. I watched my blood flowing as I might have watched a stream, without even thinking that the blood had anything to do with me. I felt throughout my whole being such a wonderful calm, that whenever I recall this feeling I can find nothing to compare with it in all the pleasures that stir our lives.[1]

It is extraordinary here that ecstasy is *not* presented as a "going out of the self," as it is always too quickly and simplistically put. On the contrary, it is expressed first as night's advance and arrival ("Night was coming on"), and then as the reception—before the author gets hold of himself or returns to himself, before even the appearance of the perceiving "I"—of this advance, which happens

by itself, and in which no "subject," in any case, has the least responsibility. And it is exactly such an advance and reception that
give the feeling of existing, a feeling that is itself anterior to any
form of self-consciousness, and so little connected with a subject
that it simultaneously reaches all earthly objects ("It seemed as if
all I perceived was filled with my frail existence"); the result, conversely, is that even the "body itself" (blood) is perceived as something belonging to the earth (a stream), and is drawn into the same
feeling of "it exists."

Rousseau's ecstasy here takes the form of what I have called, for
lack of a better word, the paradoxical experience of death; that is,
its simulation. It is why Rousseau can say "In this instant I was being born again," if, as I have attempted to articulate, death is the
pro-spect of the gift of birth. It is thus a paradoxical experience of
birth (into the world)—perhaps even of the birth *of* the world. In
the firmest possible manner, Celan calls this birth "perceiving," or
thinking, and assigns its task to poetry.

§ 8 Vertigo

March 25, 1984 (Tübingen)

With R.L. on the banks of the Neckar, near the tower.

Some time ago, René Bonargent, an engraver who produces luxury editions of books, published a collection of "quotations" from *Suite*,[1] accompanied by etchings and entitled *Tournoyer* (*Whirl*). But beyond, or rather, before anecdote, I think here of Celan's dizziness (I would learn more about this in Nice in February 1985, during a conversation with Bernard Böschenstein). I reread:

> The prisoner of a closed but unbordered space, I am sucked in by an eddy; and thus, owing to the swirling, I am brought back to a torture from which I have tried, in vain, to move away: resembling, even in my own eyes, a rambling, repetitive old man incapable of silence, and incapable myself of either taking off this mask or identifying with its character.

There is a sentence in "The Meridian" that I haven't dared touch. It says:

> Die Dichtung, meine Damen und Herren—: diese Unendlich-sprechung von lauter Sterblichkeit und Umsonst![2]

Blanchot translates:

> Poetry, Ladies and Gentlemen: the word of the infinite, the word of vain death and of sole Nothing.

Du Bouchet:

> Poetry—: a conversion into the infinite of pure mortality and the dead letter.[3]

(Why did du Bouchet systematically eliminate "Ladies and Gentlemen" from "The Meridian"?)

Jean Launay:

> Poetry, Ladies and Gentlemen—: those infinite words that treat only what is mortal and useless.[4]

And if I venture to translate:

> Poetry, Ladies and Gentlemen—: that infinite speaking of pure mortality and the in-vain.

§9 Blindness

April 13, 1984 (Barcelona)

Blindness:

> In den verfahrenen Augen—lies da:
>
> In the eyes all awry—read there:[1]

This is the first verse of the poem "Les globes," in *Die Niemandsrose*. The poem ends thus:

> Alles,
> das Schwerste noch, war
> flügge, nichts
> hielt zurück.

> All things,
> even the heaviest, were
> fledged, nothing
> held back.

It defines love.

§ 10 *Lied*

April 21, 1984 (Todtnauberg)

Heidegger:

The default of God and the divinities is absence. But absence is not nothing; rather it is precisely the presence, which must first be appropriated, of the hidden fullness and wealth of what has been and what, thus gathered, is presencing, of the divine in the world of the Greeks, in prophetic Judaism, in the preaching of Jesus. This no-longer is in itself a not-yet of the veiled arrival of its inexhaustible nature.[1]

Celan:

> Von deinem Gott war die Rede, ich sprach
> gegen ihn, ich
> liess das Herz, das ich hatte,
> hoffen:
> auf
> sein höchstes, umröcheltes, sein
> haderndes Wort—
>
> Dein Aug sah mir zu, sah hinweg,
> dein Mund
> sprach sich dem Aug zu, ich hörte:
>
> Wir
> wissen ja nicht, weisst du,

wir
wissen ja nicht,
was
gilt.

Of your God was our talk, I spoke
against him, I
let the heart that I had
hope:
for
his highest, death-rattled, his
quarrelling word—

Your eye looked on, looked away,
your mouth
spoke its way to the eye, and I heard:

We
don't know, you know,
we
don't know, do we?
what
counts.[2]

    The path indeed bears his name: Martin-Heidegger Weg (but afterward, to get to the chalet, we still have to walk across fields in the snow. The noise of the mechanical ski lift doesn't stop until about five o'clock).

    There has been much ironic commentary on the path motif: *Feldweg, Holzwege, Unterwegs, Wegmarken,* and so on. So much for rustic charm. But where in philosophy, and even outside philosophy (in Eastern thought, for example), have people pictured thought as other than a path? From Parmenides and Lao-Tzu to Heidegger. (I don't remember who told me that J.D. did a seminar on this subject, using the short text I had more or less "established" and translated with Roger Munier: "The Flaw In Sacred Names." In it, Heidegger "invents" an aphorism on Greek thought: "A path ἡ ὁδός is never a method μέθοδος.")

    Celan could not fail to think of Heidegger and the path motif

when writing "The Meridian," and even "The Bremen Speech."
Not only poetry itself (all poems), but also the thought of poetry
appear there as paths. Some people have of course objected to me
that this motif is related to Benjamin's "itineraries," to his praise of
the *flâneur* and the Baudelairian "encounter." But I do not think
this connection is correct. If Benjamin is to be found in Celan—
and he is—we should not look for him here. I remain convinced
that the "dialogue" with Heidegger is critical, at least for the issue
of poetry's essence. That is why the encounter of 1967, in this very
place, took on such importance in Celan's eyes.

From the beginning, I made a rule for myself that I would not
recount the story of this encounter and its aftermath. Or that I
would divulge only things that Celan himself had said, and that
had been recorded in various places. It is not for me to say more.
But I can at least report on a text that W.H. passed along to me:
an article that appeared—W.H. does not know when; what he gave
me was a copy of the manuscript—in the *Liechtensteinisches Volks-
blatt.*[3] The author is Robert Altmann, an editor friendly with
Celan. Prompted to write by a series of articles published in the
Züricher Zeitung in honor of Heidegger, and in particular by an article by Beda Allemann on Heidegger's relation to poetry, Altmann
simply presents the facts:

> "Todtnauberg," whose title comes from the place in the Black Forest
> where Heidegger played host to the poet in the spring of 1967, ap-
> peared in print in 1968. Earlier, I had published the *Atemkristall* col-
> lection with engravings by Gisèle Celan, and Celan expressed the wish
> to see his poem published in a small, separate edition. We chose the
> same format as that of the previous edition, and we had fifty num-
> bered copies of the bound poem printed on the hand presses at Fequet
> et Baudier in Paris. In August 1968, the edition was exhibited at the
> Raduz technical school, along with all the works published by Editions
> Brunidor. Celan came in person and gave, one evening, a reading of
> his poems. It was one of his last readings, as he took his life several
> months later.
>
> "Todtnauberg" is, strictly speaking, nothing other than a descrip-
> tion of the journey to the philosopher's house: flowers, landscape,

fountain, a trip in a car. But as always with Celan, each word hides a world of images and ideas. "Arnica, balm for the eyes" is at once an early summer field flower and a medicinal plant, the sick man's hope of cure and consolation. Water drawn from the star-crowned fountain, which is similar, we might say, to a miraculous source. But then comes the poem's central point, that Beda Allemann interprets as the expectation of the poet to come, in the sense of Kleist's poet of the future. I believe, however, that this viewpoint does not encompass Celan's intention, which was to ask, and impose, the question of the philosopher's position vis-à-vis his Hitler-era declarations. Celan writes something in the guest book about the hope that Heidegger will explicitly distance himself from his earlier attitude. That a doubt should surface following this question connected with hope is evident in the poem's description, in a sudden change of landscape: the marsh, the uneven fields, the damp and muddy paths succeed and undo the image of springtime and hope. The dialogue witnessed by the anonymous chauffeur is then transformed into a monologue, as always in Celan; he was able to create a solitary and grandiose work from the tragic imbalance of his entire life.

Heidegger's letter[4] indeed avoided the crucial question. The redeeming response failed to come. Nevertheless, for the poet this encounter was an interior experience of great importance. Poet and philosopher both strove to grasp the meaning of the total artist and total language. Celan's suffering and struggle for absolute expression led him, from that time on, to increasingly interiorized forms of writing. . . .

The poet closely oversaw the production of the "Todtnauberg." Now the poem, born of an intensely topical question, remains itself, independent of temporal circumstances. From the small bibliophile's edition, copies went only to friends and a few libraries. None was sold. It was certainly Celan's wish to cut off any kind of discussion with Heidegger. This explains, too, why nothing became public later on, as Beda Allemann notes. The theme had been transformed into a purely poetic one.[5]

Altmann's very simple description suggests that "*Todtnauberg*" is perhaps a pure *Lied.* The last?

§ 11 Sky

May 1st, 1984 (Les Ayes)

I necessarily scruple to speak about Judaism. Yet with Celan, one must. But I cannot. Not only my ignorance is at issue. It is more a question of propriety.

Thus, I can approach only negatively the element of Celan's poetry that clearly proceeds from the Jewish tradition, the essence that is probably only readable with an understanding of that tradition. For example, everything I have painfully tried to articulate on poetry as prayer aims solely to measure the distance between the (so-called, clearly non-existent) "theology" Heidegger asks of Hölderlin, and the question of God that haunts Celan's poetry, perhaps to the very end.

Perhaps to the very end; I think of the poem in the final collection, *Zeitgehöft* (*Farmstead of Time*), that so clearly responds, still and again, to Hölderlin:

> Ich trink Wein aus zwei Gläsern
> und zackere an
> wie Jener
> am Pindar,
>
> Gott gibt die Stimmgabel ab
> als einer der kleinen
> Gerechten,

aus der Lostrommel fällt
unser Deut.

I drink wine from two glasses
and comb through
the king's caesura
like that one
with Pindar,

God turns over the tuning-fork
alone of the small
just ones,

from the fate-engine falls
our measure.[1]

I tried to translate the poem several years ago. I gave up, not knowing how to render *Deut*, offered in the English as "measure." *Deut*, which survives only in fixed expressions (for example, *um keinen Deut besser*, "not one whit better"), means something insignificant or trifling: a near nothing. The poem takes up the Hölderlinian question of measure and the law, the question of the poem "In Lovely Blueness": Is there a measure on earth? Or the one Hölderlin illuminates in the fragment of Pindar entitled "Das Höchste" ("The Highest"), which he restitutes thus:

Das Gesez,
Von allen der König, Sterblichen und
Unsterblichen; das führt eben
Darum gewaltig
Das gerechteste Recht mit allerhöchster Hand.[2]

The law,
King of all, mortals and
Immortals; it indeed drives
Powerfully, for that reason,
Justice most just with the highest hand.

The "response" to Hölderlin is that of Jewish messianism. Was it in Buber, Scholem, or Benjamin that I read, a long while back, this parable of the Messiah? He is there, always, at every instant; or rather, he was always there just an instant ago: the beggar who just left the room or the little man who just turned the street corner. Measure, what sets the tone, is not Pindar's Δίχη, but the just man, the just little man. God is still the one who metes measure out, but almost in the way one might get rid of something. And what falls in the way of destiny is insignificant. But that is just the point . . .

Where can the distance between the two poets best be measured? First, of course, in Celan's elimination of all reference to the sacred. Everything Heidegger was able to construct from two verses of "Wie Wenn Am Feiertage" ("As On A Holiday"),

> Jetzt aber tagts! Ich harrt und sah es kommen,
> Und was ich sah, das Heilige sei mein Wort.

> But now day breaks! I waited and saw it come,
> And what I saw, the hallowed, my word shall convey.[3]

is foreign—though not *absolutely* foreign—to Celan. Not *absolutely* foreign is the designation of the "sacred" (a word which to my knowledge he never used) as the Open (chaos, gaping, wild vastness). Celan, too, speaks in this direction. The allusion to Pindar's "king's caesura" is quite clear: an allusion to the impossible immediacy, or more exactly the impossible immediate attainment of immediacy (the Open), which is nevertheless the very mediation in, and origin of, any kind of relation.[4] But for Celan, the Open is not the sacred, and poetry's task is not "to name the sacred." First, no doubt, because the sacred is not "the element of the divine."[5] In this sense the experience of the sacred is absolutely foreign to Celan.

But that is relatively secondary. Something much more crucial is at issue, or at least, something that does not simply participate in the facile (and easily utilized) opposition between Greek "paganism"—polytheism—and Jewish monotheism. (For conceiving the divine, the God or God, the opposition is perhaps without consequence. And for belief and faith, I wonder if the same isn't true; I wonder too if Christianity, because it is essentially founded on this opposition, is not ultimately responsible for our "atheism.")

Could anything be more crucial?

The question, perhaps *everywhere* present, of man's resemblance to (the) God.

Heidegger makes this the topic of a long commentary that forms the lecture "dichterisch wohnet der Mensch" ("Poetically Man Dwells")[6]—a lecture, as it happens, on "In Lieblicher Bläue" ("In Lovely Blueness") and on the question, as it happens, of measure. The verses Heidegger analyzes are the following:

> Darf, wenn lauter Mühe das Leben, ein Mensch aufschauen und sagen: so will ich auch seyn? Ja. Solange die Freundlichkeit noch am Herzen, die Reine, dauert, misset nicht unglüklich der Mensch sich mit der Gottheit. Ist unbekannt Gott? Ist er offenbar wie der Himmel? Dieses glaub' ich eher. Des Menschen Maass ist's. Voll Verdienst, doch dichterisch, wohnet der Mensch auf dieser Erde. Doch reiner ist nicht der Schatten der Nacht mit den Sternen, wenn ich so sagen könnte, als der Mensch, der heisset ein Bild der Gottheit. Giebt es auf Erden ein Maass? Es giebt keines.

> May, when life is all trouble, may a man
> Look upwards and say: I
> Also would like to be thus? Yes. As long
> As kindness,[7] which is pure, lasts in his heart,
> Man not unhappily can measure himself
> With the divine. Is God unknown?
> Is He visible as the sky? This
> I rather believe. It's the measure of men.
> Full of merit[8] but poetically man
> Lives on this earth. But the shadow
> Of night with the stars is not purer,
> If I could put it like that, than
> Man, who is called the image of God.
> Is there a measure on earth? There is
> None.[9]

Radically reducing Heidegger's "demonstration" to its structural impetus establishes that:

1. In lifting his gaze toward the sky and its inhabitants, man—whose life, otherwise, is "all trouble" and in that sense "full of merit"—"measures all the distance that separates us from the sky," that is, "all that is between sky and earth." The distance, the space between, is what Heidegger calls the Dimension, which he considers the origin of the very relation between sky and earth, and thus, the origin of space as such and of human habitation. Man's term on earth starts with the Dimension. (Of course, that is not where the difference lies. I mean that this other opposition, between habitation on one hand—Greek, German, and so on—and wandering and nomadism on the other—Jews, and others—is also weak. Dwelling, being *zuhause*, is, for example, Celan's primary preoccupation.)

2. The pre-eminent means of taking the measure—according to "his own μέτρου" and "thus also his own metrics"—is poetry. It opens man's term on earth as inhabiting, or living, "as a poet." But for poetry, taking the measure is always "relating to something celestial" and measuring oneself with it: "Man not unhappily can measure himself / With the divine." Man takes the measure, not from the earth itself ("Is there a measure on earth? There is / None."), but, inasmuch as this gives his measure as a mortal being (able to die), from the Divinity. The measure is "the Divinity with which man measures himself."

3. The Divinity, or rather God, is the measure in that he is unknown. Here Heidegger analyzes the central passage of the verses he extracted from the poem:

The question begins in line 29 with the words: "Is God unknown?" Manifestly not. For if he were unknown, how could he, being unknown, ever be the measure? Yet—and this is what we must now listen to and keep in mind—for Hölderlin God, as the one who he is, is unknown and it is just as *this Unknown One* that he is the measure for the poet. This is also why Hölderlin is perplexed by the exciting question: how can that which by its very nature remains unknown ever become a measure? For something that man measures himself by must after all impart itself, must appear. But if it appears, it is known. The god, however, is unknown, and he is the measure nonetheless. Not only this, but the god who remains unknown, must by showing *himself* as the one he is, appear as the one who remains unknown. God's *manifestness*—not only he himself—is mysterious. Therefore the poet immediately asks the next question: "Is he manifest like the sky?" Hölderlin answers: "I'd sooner / Believe the latter."[10]

Why—so *we* now ask—is the poet's surmise inclined in that way? The very next words give the answer. They say tersely: "It's the measure of man." What is the measure for human measuring? God? No. The sky? No. The manifestness of the sky? No. The measure consists in the way in which the god who remains unknown, is revealed *as* such by the sky. God's appearance through the sky consists in a disclosing that lets us see what conceals itself, but lets us see it not by seeking to wrest what is concealed out of its concealedness, but only by guarding the concealed in its self-concealment. Thus the unknown god appears as the unknown by way of the sky's manifestness. This appearance is the measure against which man measures himself.[11]

This analysis is surprising.

Surprising, because on one hand it recognizes the absolute paradox of God's manifestation, or more exactly his revelation (*Offenbarkeit*, Hölderlin's question being "Ist er offenbar wie der Himmel?"): "At the same time he shows himself as the one He is," God appears "as the one who remains unknown." God thus reveals himself as not revealing himself in appearing or manifestation. The revelation is not an appearance. If Heidegger's reading is correct, if Hölderlin's "rather"—"This I rather believe"—is not a restriction as to the unknown being of God, it means: God, the unknown, shows himself as the sky does; he is as manifest as the sky. But it is the (sky's) manifestation that is enigmatic. For how is the sky manifest, if not here—"In Lovely Blueness"—as the pure void of bottomless light, the pure spacing, above our heads, of air and light (Ether); the spacing that outlines, rather than being outlined by, the earth; the spacing, out of which the earth's space spreads and all things become visible, articulate themselves? God shows or reveals himself in the same way as the sky's pure opening—the "abyss," as Celan would say; as the ceaseless ebb, on and right against the whole surface of the visible, the invisible from which the visible streams. And even when the sky shows itself in its "qualities," as Hölderlin says in another poem,[12] light's luminosity continues to withdraw to it as its very appearance.

But if Heidegger reads something of this order in Hölderlin—which is probable, given the connection he makes to the poem "What is God?"[13]—then it is impossible to say that for Hölderlin, "the measure consists in the way in which the god who remains unknown, is revealed as such, by the sky (*durch den Himmel*)." Hölderlin does *not* say that God shows himself "by way of the sky," but rather, to express it a bit differently, that he is evident as the invisible is evident, withdrawn into the visible *as* its visibility. Hölderlin's thought is here unrelated to, say, Hegel's: *Das Offenbarte ist nur dass Gott der Offenbare ist.* This does not mean, as people are in the habit of translating, "The revealed is simply that God can be revealed," but instead, "The revealed (that which is revealed) is simply that God is the revealed (the manifest)." Whereas Hegel conceives revelation's perfect being-in-evidence, Hölderlin thinks of its abyss. This, in fact, is why the logic animating the verses—

> What sends itself into strangeness
> Is all the more invisible

—is completely unconnected to dialectics. Despite all appearances to the contrary. Unlike the Hegelian Absolute, God, for Hölderlin, does not want "to be at our side." But the more he sends himself into "the sky's aspect," which is unknown to him, the more he "reveals" himself as invisible. Thus Heidegger can say: "The poet calls, in the sights of the sky, that which in its very self-disclosure causes the appearance of that which conceals itself, and indeed *as* that which conceals itself. In the familiar appearance, the poet calls the alien as that to which the invisible imparts itself in order to remain what it is—unknown."[14] But then it suddenly becomes clear, and makes Heidegger's analysis surprising for a second time, that the structure of the revelation is none other than that of *aletheia* itself; hence, in a mode doubtless no longer metaphysical, the onto-theological risk is still present, and all the more so when God is conceived from the initial question *"what* is God?" It is perhaps this onto-theological horizon that forces Heidegger, in the very gesture he uses to remove the whole problematic of imitation from his commentary (a problematic which is, however, explicit in the poem) to define taking the measure not as the imitation of "reserve" or divine retreat, but as the image-rich language of poetry that "makes us see the Invisible":

> The poet makes poetry only when he takes the measure, by saying the sights of heaven in such a way that he submits to its appearances as to the alien element to which the unknown god has "yielded." Our current name for the sight and appearance of something is "image" (*Bild*). The nature of the image is to let something be seen. By contrast, copies and imitations are already mere variations on the genuine image which, as a sight or spectacle, lets the invisible be seen and so imagines the invisible in something alien to it. Because poetry takes that mysterious measure, to wit, in the face of the sky, therefore it speaks in "images." This is why poetic images are imaginings (*Ein-bildungen*) in a distinctive sense: not mere fancies and illusions but imaginings that are visible inclusions of the alien in the sight of the familiar.[15]

I am not saying that "In Lovely Blueness" is not haunted by images.[16] I would say, rather, that we should try to think about the relationship—clear in both French and English through Latin—between image and imitation. And especially that we should understand what Hölderlin envisions when he thinks of man as "an image of God." The lines Heidegger extracts immediately follow this passage:

> Reinheit aber ist auch Schönheit. Innen aus Verschiedenem entsteht ein ernster Geist. So sehr einfältig die Bilder, so sehr.
> Heilig sind die, dass man wirklich oft fürchtet, die zu beschreiben. Die Himmlischen aber, die immer gut sind, alles zumal, wie Reiche, haben diese Tugend und Freude. Der Mensch darf das nachahmen. Darf, wenn lauter Mühe das Leben, ein Mensch . . .

> > But
> > Pureness is also beauty.

Within, divergence creates a serious spirit.
But pictures are so simple, so holy
Are these that really one is
Often afraid to describe them. But the heavenly,
Who are always good, all at once, like the rich,
Have this virtue and pleasure. Man
May imitate that.
May, when life is all trouble, may a man . . . [17]

This is also the measure for Hölderlin: kindness, *Freundlichkeit,* as the imitation of divine goodness—virtue and pleasure; it shows itself as the sky, that is, as light's modesty—in its very nudity—and as the jubilation of reserving the visible in the self. What is lacking is the "source": grace—as kindness is reserved. God *is* not (absent). He goes away. He lets man die, lets him be human, leaves him kindness in the capacity to die. Something like love, then; what God gives in withdrawing from mortals' desire (will), which is always to be immortal (but this should again be understood in the context of Hölderlin's "atheism," and in any case without reference to who knows what kind of "Swabian piety").

Imitating the divine means two things: wanting to be God (the Greek tragic experience), and "humbly" keeping God's retreat as a model (the "Western" experience—just as tragic, but in another sense).

The distance between them is measured here. A poem in *Sprachgitter* says this (changing the direction of prayer in the name of a carnal proximity between the God and man, in order to signify that God's image is man's blood shed: God present, which is to say withdrawn, not in "the figure of death," but in the face of the dead—the exterminated):

TENEBRAE

Nah sind wir, Herr,
nahe und greifbar.

Gegriffen schon, Herr,
ineinander verkrallt, als wär
der Leib eines jeden von uns
dein Leib, Herr.

Bete, Herr,
bete zu uns,
wir sind nah.

Windscheif gingen wir hin,
gingen wir hin, uns zu bücken
nach Mulde und Maar.

Zur Tränke gingen wir, Herr.

Es war Blut, es war,
was du vergossen, Herr.

Es glänzte.

Es warf uns dein Bild in die Augen, Herr.
Augen und Mund stehn so offen und leer, Herr.
Wir haben getrunken, Herr.
Das Blut und das Bild, das im Blut war, Herr.

Bete, Herr.
Wir sind nah.

We are near, Lord,
near and at hand.

Handled already, Lord,
clawed and clawing as though
the body of each of us were
your body, Lord.

Pray, Lord,
pray to us,
we are near.

Wind-awry we went there,
went there to bend
over hollow and ditch.

To be watered we went there, Lord.

It was blood, it was
what you shed, Lord.

It gleamed.

It cast your image into our eyes, Lord.
Our eyes and our mouths are so open and empty, Lord.
We have drunk, Lord.
The blood and the image that was in the blood, Lord.

Pray, Lord.
We are near.[18]

§ 12 The Unforgivable

August 4, 1984 (Genoa)

C.F. says he was told—by a French intellectual, I think—that French intellectuals harp too much on the pathos of Auschwitz (Auschwitz as understood by Adorno, George Steiner, and several others who can hardly be classified as French intellectuals). If we start to forget this, the unthinkable—that it happened here, that our brothers (our fellow men) let it happen, that they said nothing, were afraid, felt some degree of enjoyment, and that it was pure monstrosity—if we start no longer to understand in what ways it was pure monstrosity, then I hold out little hope for the future of thought, or, in any case, for those who imagine themselves "intelligent" in saying such things. The most one can wish them is to avoid "pathos" on lesser "subjects."

Herein lies Heidegger's irreparable offense: not in his declarations of 1933–34, which we can understand without approving, but in his silence on the extermination. He should have been the first to say something. And I was wrong to think initially that it was enough to ask forgiveness. It is absolutely *unforgivable.* That is what he should have said. In any case, there is a risk that thought will never recover from such silence:

> Τῷ πάθει μάθος
> To learn to know through pain . . .
> *(Aeschylus,* Agamemnon*)*

Pain:

> No, it is not I, it is someone else who suffers.
> I, I could not have suffered thus.
>
> *(Anna Akhmatova,* Requiem*)*

Reference Matter

Notes

Part I

1. ["Der Meridian" is in volume 3 of Celan's five-volume *Gesammelte Werke*, ed. Beda Allemann and Stefan Reichert, in collaboration with Rolf Bücher (Frankfurt: Suhrkamp, 1983). This passage, p. 200. Unless otherwise noted, all English translations from "Der Meridian" are from Jerry Glenn's "The Meridian," in *Chicago Review* 29, no. 3 (1978): 29–40. This passage, p. 38.—Trans.]

2. [*GW* 1: 226. English translations of Celan's poems will be Michael Hamburger's unless otherwise noted. "Tübingen, Jänner" is in *Paul Celan: Poems* (New York: Persea, 1988), 177.—Trans.]

3. [*GW* 2: 25; Hamburger, *Celan*, 293.—Trans.]

4. [Apart from Michael Hamburger's translations of both poems, there is an English version of *Tübingen, Jänner* in Joachim Neugroschel, *Paul Celan, Speech-Grille* (New York: E. P. Dutton, 1971), 185.—Trans.]

5. [Lacoue-Labarthe's phrase is "c'est avec l'Allemagne qu'il faut . . . s'expliquer." *S'expliquer* in this context means primarily "to discuss," "to clarify matters," even "to have it out with someone." Yet the verb could also function as a simple reflexive; this would render the sense, "We must explain *ourselves* with Germany." The import of such ambiguity for reflections on the Holocaust is self-evident.—Trans.]

6. [From "Todesfuge": "der Tod ist ein Meister aus Deutschland." *GW* 1: 42; "Death Fugue," Hamburger, *Celan*, 63.—Trans.]

7. Henri Meschonnic, "On appelle cela traduire Celan," in *Pour la poétique II* (Paris: Gallimard, 1980).

8. *GW* 2: 334. Peter Szondi, "Eden," in *Poésies et poétiques de la modernité* (Lille: Presses universitaires de Lille, 1981).

9. Issues 2 and 3, 1972. Blanchot, *Le dernier à parler*, was reissued by fata morgana in Paris in 1984.

10. Theodor Adorno, "Parataxe," in *Notes to Literature*, vol. 2, trans. Shierry Weber Nicholson (New York: Columbia University Press, 1991), 109–49.

11. Along with, in an entirely different vein, Werner Hamacher, "The Second of Inversion: Movements of a Figure Through Celan's Poetry," trans. Peter Fenves, in *Word Traces: Readings of Paul Celan*, ed. Aris Fioretos (Baltimore, Md.: Johns Hopkins University Press, 1994), 219–63.

12. [The French "tour / noyées" plays on a double meaning: the verb *tournoyer* can be translated as "to wheel around, whirl, swirl," while dividing the past participle of the verb into two parts evokes "tower / drowned."—Trans.]

13. [It is worth stressing that this English version translates Lacoue-Labarthe's French translation, rather than Celan's German.—Trans.]

14. Friedrich Hölderlin, *Sämtliche Werke*, vol. 2.1 (Stuttgart: Kohlhammer, 1951), 195.

15. I refer the reader to Roger Munier (responding to an inquiry on experience in *Mise en page* 1 [May 1972]): "First there is etymology. *Experience* comes from the Latin *experiri*, to test, try, prove. The radical is *periri*, which one also finds in *periculum*, peril, danger. The Indo-European root is *per*, to which are attached the ideas of *crossing* and, secondarily, of *trial, test*. In Greek, numerous derivations evoke a crossing or passage: *peirô*, to cross; *pera*, beyond; *peraô*, to pass through; *perainô*, to go to the end; *peras*, end, limit. For Germanic languages, Old High German *faran* has given us *fahren*, to transport, and *führen*, to drive. Should we attribute *Erfahrung* to this origin as well, or should it be linked to the second meaning of *per*, trial, in Old High German *fara*, danger, which became *Gefahr*, danger, and *gefährden*, to endanger? The boundaries between one meaning and the other are imprecise. The same is true for the Latin *periri*, to try, and *periculum*, which originally means trial, test, then risk, danger. The idea of experience as a crossing is etymologically and semantically difficult to separate from that of risk. From the beginning and no doubt in a fundamental sense, *experience* means to endanger."

16. The French translation I will refer to is not André du Bouchet's in *Strette* (Paris: Mercure de France, 1971), but Jean Launay's (*Po&sie* 9

[1979]). I make slight modifications when the argument warrants. [For this passage, see Glenn, 37: "The poem is . . . underway."—Trans.]

17. [In the original, this line reads "Ein Räthsel ist Reinentsprungenes." In English, Michael Hamburger renders it "An enigma are things of pure source"; see *Hölderlin: His Poems* (New York: Pantheon, 1952), 199. I have modified the English translation because of Lacoue-Labarthe's repeated use of *jailli* and *jaillissement.*—Trans.]

18. [In English, agitation or excitement.—Trans.]

19. Walter Benjamin, *Charles Baudelaire, Ein Lyriker im Zeitalter des Hochkapitalismus,* in *Gesammelte Schriften,* vol. 1.2, ed. Rolf Tiedemann and Hermann Schweppenhäuser (Frankfurt am Main: Suhrkamp, 1974). English references: *Charles Baudelaire: A Lyric Poet in the Era of High Capitalism,* trans. Harry Zohn (London: NLB, 1973).

20. [*GW* 2: 36.—Trans.]

21. Benjamin, "Über einige Motive bei Baudelaire," *Schriften,* 1.2: 605–53; "Some Motifs in Baudelaire," *Charles Baudelaire,* 107–54.

22. [Celan's Bremen address is published in the *GW* 3: 186. The English translation cited here is by Rosmarie Waldrop, in *Paul Celan: Collected Prose* (Manchester, England: Carcanet Press, 1986), 33.—Trans.]

23. The lectures on Hölderlin, now published by Klostermann in Heidegger's *Gesamtausgabe.* The better part of Heidegger's essays or papers on Hölderlin presuppose knowledge of these lectures.

24. See Beda Allemann's commentary in *Hölderlin et Heidegger* (Paris: P.U.F., 1959).

25. [Hölderlin, *SW* 2.1: 190–92. Trans. Michael Hamburger, *Friedrich Hölderlin: Poems and Fragments* (Cambridge: Cambridge University Press, 1980), 495.—Trans.]

26. "Anmerkungen zum 'Ödipus'" in *SW* 5: 196; "Remarks on 'Oedipus,'" in *Friedrich Hölderlin: Essays and Letters on Theory,* trans. Thomas Pfau (Albany: SUNY Press, 1988), 107.

27. I have attempted this analysis in "La césure du spéculatif" (in Hölderlin, *L'Antigone de Sophocle* [Paris: Bourgois, 1978]) and in "Hölderlin et les Grecs" (*Poétique* 40 [1979]).

28. Jean Beaufret, "Hölderlin et Sophocle," in Hölderlin, *Remarques sur Oedipe—Remarques sur Antigone* (Paris: U.G.E., 1965).

29. [Hamburger, *Hölderlin,* 601.—Trans.]

30. [Hamburger, *Celan,* 175.—Trans.]

31. [Hölderlin, *SW* 2.1: 146; Hamburger, *Hölderlin,* 417.—Trans.]

32. [Hölderlin, *SW* 2.1: 13; Hamburger, *Hölderlin,* 131.—Trans.]

33. [Glenn, 33.—Trans.]

34. [Arthur Rimbaud, *Oeuvres II: Vers nouveaux, Une saison en enfer* (Paris: Garnier-Flammarion, 1989), 57; *Rimbaud: Complete Works, Selected Letters*, trans. Wallace Fowlie (Chicago: University of Chicago Press, 1966), 125.—Trans.]

35. [Glenn, 35–37.—Trans.]

36. [Ibid., 36.—Trans.]

37. [Ibid., 32; *GW* 3: 192.—Trans.]

38. "Die Ros' ist ohne warum; sie blühet, weil sie blühet; / Sie acht' nicht ihrer selbst, fragt nicht, ob man sie siehet": "The rose is without a why, blooms because it blooms; / Has no care for itself, nor desires to be seen." See Heidegger, *Satz vom Grund* (Pfullingen: Neske, 1957), and *The Principle of Reason*, trans. Reginald Lilly (Bloomington: Indiana University Press,1991).

39. [Glenn, 34; *GW* 3: 195.—Trans.]

40. [Glenn, 35; *GW* 3: 195.—Trans.]

41. *SW* 4.1: 233.

42. [*Paul Celan*, trans. Waldrop, 18–19.—Trans.]

43. Blanchot, *Le Dernier à parler*, 45.

44. *GW* 3: 185–6; *Paul Celan*, Waldrop, 34.

Catastrophe

1. ["Stammering" translates the French *bégaiement*, which corresponds to Celan's *lallen* in "Tübingen, Jänner" (*GW* 1: 226). Michael Hamburger translates *lallen* as "babble" (*Celan*, 177).—Trans.]

2. [*GW* 3: 202; Glenn, 40. In this section, page references to "The Meridian" will be given in the main body of the text: first to the German, then to Glenn's English translation, and last to the French translation by Jean Launay used by Lacoue-Labarthe ("'Le Méridien.' Discours prononcé à l'occasion de la remise du prix Georg Büchner," *Poésie* 9 (1979): 68–82. At times, the English translation has been modified, in particular to coincide with Lacoue-Labarthe's use of Launay's French version of Celan's text.—Trans.]

3. The acceptance speech for the Georg Büchner Prize customarily addresses Büchner's work.

4. "Une lecture de Paul Celan," *Poésie* 9 (1979): 7.

5. In the same issue of *Poésie*, Launay includes, along with his translations of "The Meridian" and the scenes from *Dantons Tod* it refers to,

translations of Kafka's "Ein Bericht für eine Akademie," *Gesammelte Werke in sieben Bänden* (Frankfurt: Hanser, 1983), and Egon Friedell's *Talents zur Wahrheit* (1910), in order to clarify the tone proper to "The Meridian."

6. [Glenn's translation of "The Meridian" gives three different versions of *Atemwende*: "reversal of breath," "turn of breath," and "breath turning."—Trans.]

7. "Pas (préambule)," in *Gramma* 3–4 (1976).[This text is reprinted in Jacques Derrida, *Parages* (Paris: Galilée, 1986), 19–116. *Pas* in French means both "step" and "not."—Trans.]

8. [This is Lacoue-Labarthe's first mention of *propre*, a word to which he will frequently return. I have given it in English as "own," or, when possible, as "proper."—Trans.]

9. [*Dantons Tod*, in Georg Büchner's *Werke und Briefe*, ed. Fritz Bergemann (Wiesbaden: Insel, 1949), 41; *The Death of Danton*, trans. Howard Brenton and Jane Fry, in Georg Büchner, *The Complete Plays*, ed. Michael Patterson (London: Methuen, 1987), 40.—Trans.]

10. Connections should be made here between the commentary on Sophocles in Martin Heidegger, *Einführung in die Metaphysik* (Tübingen: Niemeyer, 1953), and the 1942 lectures on "Der Ister," in Martin Heidegger, *Hölderlins Hymne "Der Ister"* (Frankfurt: Klostermann, 1984); "Der Ursprung des Kunstwerkes," in Martin Heidegger, *Holzwege* (Frankfurt: Klostermann, 1950), 7–68; and the "Brief über den Humanismus," in Martin Heidegger, *Wegmarken* (Frankfurt: Klostermann, 1967), 145–94 (the passage on the translation of Heraclitus's maxim, *ethos anthrope daimon* [185–94]).

11. Or when, on the contrary—but it amounts to exactly the same thing—he seems to appropriate the *Unheimliche* as the "realm in which the monkey, the robots, and accordingly . . . alas, art, too, seem to be at home" (192; 32; 72).

12. [Lacoue-Labarthe's words are "quelque chose . . . se renverse," with *renverser* as the echo of "catastrophe" (from the Greek *katastrephein*, "to turn down," "overturn"). Although I have used "overturn" here, the three other instances in which a form of *renverser* occurs seem to require "upset."—Trans.]

13. Once again we are very close to Hölderlin—"language, that most dangerous of possessions," and even to the Heideggerian interpretation of this phrase. See "Hölderlin und das Wesen der Dichtung," in Martin Heidegger, *Erläuterungen zu Hölderlins Dichtung* (Frankfurt: Kloster-

mann, 1981), 33–45. Heidegger thinks of danger as that which threatens
Being rather than the human. But Hölderlin's phrase derives from a
fragment that seeks to respond to the question: "Who is man?" As for
Celan's determination of the human, what would it be without relation
to Being, that is—I will come to this—to time? Even if "The Meridian"
is, as we may plausibly allow, partially addressed to Heidegger, that is
not sufficient reason to hastily read into it an "ethical" response to "ontology." The human is in no way an "ethical" category, and moreover,
no category of this kind can resist the question of Being. [Lacoue-
Labarthe quotes Hölderlin from the fragment "Im Walde," in *SW* 2.1:
325. Cf. "In the Forest," in Friedrich Hölderlin, *Hymns and Fragments*,
trans. Richard Sieburth (Princeton, N.J.: Princeton University Press,
1984), 57.—Trans.]

14. "Anmerkungen zum 'Ödipus,'" in *SW* 5: 196; "Remarks on 'Oedipus,'" in Thomas Pfau, trans., *Essays and Letters on Theory*, 102.

15. Jean-Luc Nancy's term. See *Le discours de la syncope* (Paris: Aubier-
Flammarion, 1976).

16. [Hölderlin, "Anmerkungen zum 'Ödipus,'" 196; Pfau, "Remarks
on 'Oedipus,'" 102.—Trans.]

17. ["Anmerkungen zur 'Antigona,'" in *SW* 5: 269; "Remarks on 'Antigone,'" in Pfau, *Essays and Letters on Theory*, 113.—Trans.]

18. Büchner, *Dantons Tod*, 86; Brenton and Fry, *The Death of Danton*, 80.

19. This is the case in the quatrain Celan quotes at the end of "The
Meridian":

> Voices from the path of the nettles
> *Come on your hands to us.*
> Whoever is alone with the lamp
> has only his palm to read from.
> (*GW* 3: 201)

20. Celan's words are: " . . . when I attempted to make for that distant
but occupiable realm which became visible only in the form of Lucile"
(200; 38; 80).

21. [In French, *poésie de circonstance*. There is further reference to circumstance later on.—Trans.]

22. [The translation is taken from Brian Lynch and Peter Jankowsky,
Paul Celan: 65 Poems. (Dublin: Raven Arts, 1985), 41.—Trans.]

23. [The phrase is *hen diapheron eauto*. See *Hyperion*, pt. 1, bk. 2, in

SW 3: 81. Cf. Heraclitus, fragment S1, in *Die Fragmente der Vorsokratiker*, trans. Hermann Diels, ed. Walther Kranz, 5th ed. (Berlin: Weidmann, 1934), 1: 162.—Trans.]

24. [*GW* 1: 218; Hamburger, *Celan*, 161.—Trans.]

25. [*GW* 1: 219; Hamburger, *Celan*, 163.—Trans.]

26. These are the last words of "Die Frage der Technik," in *Vorträge und Aufsätze* (Pfullingen: Neske, 1954), 36. Heidegger defines this piety as "Weise, in der das Denken dem Zu-Denkenden *entspricht.*" In this way, it is itself a product of dialogue (*Gespräch*) as the essence of language (of thought). See "Hölderlin und das Wesen der Dichtung," 38–40. Celan himself thinks of perception and questioning as dialogue.

27. [*GW* 1: 217; Hamburger, *Celan*, 159.—Trans.]

28. [A play on the title of Emmanuel Lévinas's *Autrement qu'être ou au-delà de l'essence* (Haag: Nijhoff, 1974).—Trans.]

29. *Sein und Zeit*, 11th ed. (Tübingen: Niemeyer, 1967), 38.

30. The denunciation concludes "Was ist Metaphysik?," in *Wegmarken*, 19. The problematization is in "Protokoll zu einem Seminar über den Vortrag 'Zeit und Sein,'" in Martin Heidegger, *Zur Sache des Denkens* (Tübingen: Niemeyer, 1969), 54.

31. Cf. "Über Sprache überhaupt und über die Sprache des Menschen," in *Gesammelte Schriften* (Frankfurt: Suhrkamp, 1977), 2.1: 140–57; "On Language as Such and on the Language of Man," in Walter Benjamin, *Reflections*, ed. Peter Demetz, trans. Edmund Jephcott (New York: Schocken, 1986), 314–32.

32. Walter Benjamin, "Über einige Motive bei Baudelaire," *Gesammelte Schriften*, 1.2: 639; "On Some Motifs in Baudelaire," in Walter Benjamin, *Illuminations*, ed. Hannah Arendt, trans. Harry Zohn (New York: Schocken, 1969), 199. The quotation from Valéry is from *Autres Rhumbs*.

33. [Hölderlin, *SW* 2.1: 126–29; Hölderlin, "At the Source of the Danube," in Sieburth, *Hymns and Fragments*, 57.—Trans.]

34. *GW* 1: 213; Hamburger, *Celan*, 155.

Prayer

1. [*GW* 1: 225; Hamburger, *Celan*, 175.—Trans.]

2. [Lacoue-Labarthe's phrase is "en *n*'invoquant personne"; he thus stresses that *personne* in French means both "no one" and "anyone." "Invoquer personne" would mean to invoke no one, with "no one" func-

tioning as if it were a name; "N'invoquer personne" means not to invoke anyone.—Trans.]

3. [L.-L. writes: "Dieu s'est révélé (n')être personne." See note 2 above on possible meanings for "personne."—Trans.]

4. [The Latin connects to the French word *néant,* or "nothingness."—Trans.]

5. [L.-L.'s text reads "aucun *être* en tout cas qui fût sur le mode d'un *étant*" (emphasis added).—Trans.]

6. *GW* 1: 211; Hamburger, *Celan,* 153.

7. "Typographie" in *Mimesis désarticulations* (Paris: Aubier-Flammarion, 1975). English references: "Typography," in *Typography: Mimesis, Philosophy, Politics,* ed. Christopher Fynsk (Cambridge: Harvard University Press, 1989).

8. *Fragments de Pindare,* "Das Höchste," *SW* 5: 285.

9. [In English, the play ends thus: " . . . we'll . . . ask God for macaroni, melons, and figs, for musical voices, classical bodies, and a comfortable religion!" Georg Büchner, *Leonce and Lena,* in *Complete Works and Letters,* trans. Henry J. Schmidt (New York: Continuum, 1986), 192.—Trans.]

10. [Celan's text reads " . . . ich muss mich hüten, wie *mein hier wiedergefundener Landsmann Karl Emil Franzos,* das 'Commode', das nun gebraucht wird, als ein 'Kommendes' zu lesen!" (*GW* 3: 202). Glenn translates "Commode" as "accommodating" (Glenn, 39), but I have modified this to "comfortable," in deference to the English translation of Büchner (see note 9).—Trans.]

11. [Brian Lynch and Peter Jankowsky translate the poem thus:

TWO-HOUSED, ETERNAL ONE, you are, un-
inhabitable. Therefore
we build and we build. Therefore
it stands, this
pitiful bedstead,—in the rain,
there it stands.

Come, lover.
That we lie here, that
is the partition—: He
then is sufficient unto Himself, twice.

Let Him, He
may have Himself wholly, as the half
and once again the half. We,

we are the rain-bed, may
He come and render us dry.

He comes not, He does not render us dry.

Paul Celan: 65 Poems (Dublin: Raven Arts, 1985), 36.—Trans.]

12. Glenn, 35–36.

13. At least, if the "place" of being and the *Da* of *Dasein* are substantialized, or sacralized, as has indeed been the case. In *The Experience of Thought* Heidegger writes: "But thinking poetry is in truth the topology of Being. / It says to Being the place where it unfolds." *Gesamtausgabe*, vol. 13, *Die Erfahrung des Denkens* (Frankfurt: Klosterman, 1983), 84. Celan's u-topia responds to Heidegger's topology, pushing it to its limits.

14. [*GW* 1: 217; Hamburger, *Celan*, 159.—Trans.]

15. [*GW* 1: 239–40; Hamburger, *Celan*, 187–89.—Trans.]

16. [*GW* 1: 214. The English version of the poem is Hamburger's, p. 157. However, I have had to modify the third verse of Hamburger's translation in the interest of Lacoue-Labarthe's argument. In the French translation of "Zürich, Zum Storchen" that L.-L. prints, the *Aber-Du* of the third verse has been rendered as *Non-Toi*; Hamburger gives it in English as "You-Again." I have replaced "You-Again" with "Not-You" so as to keep the filiation from the French clear for L.-L.'s subsequent remarks.—Trans.]

17. [*GW* 2: 328; Hamburger, 315.—Trans.]

18. [*GW* 2: 326. I have modified the English translation found in *Last Poems: Paul Celan*, trans. Katharine Washburn and Margret Guillemin (San Francisco: North Point, 1986), 101. Washburn and Guillemin give "rid of death, rid / of God" for Celan's "Todes quitt, Gottes / quitt"; their adjective perhaps lends a different tone to the verses from that of the French version Lacoue-Labarthe uses: "quitte de la mort, quitte / de Dieu." I have used "clear" to remain in line with Lacoue-Labarthe's reading.—Trans.]

19. [Hamburger, 315.—Trans.]

20. Böschenstein, "Destitutions," in *La revue de belles lettres* 2 (1972), 187.

Hagiography

1. [I have followed de Launay's French version as closely as possible for this English rendering. It is thus a translation of a translation, rather than a translation of Celan.—Trans.]

Pain

1. [German: "Das Wesen der Sprache" in Heidegger, *Unterwegs zur Sprache*, vol. 12 of *Gesamtausgabe* (Frankfurt: Klostermann, 1985), 159. English translation by Peter D. Hertz, in the essay "The Nature of Language," in *On the Way to Language* (San Francisco: Harper & Row, 1971), 66.—Trans.]

2. [Heidegger, *Unterwegs*, 149; Hertz, *On the Way to Language*, 57.—Trans.]

3. [Heidegger, *Unterwegs*, 222; Hertz, *On the Way to Language*, 153.—Trans.]

4. ["Die Sprache," in Heidegger, *Unterwegs*, 24; "Language," in Heidegger, *Poetry, Language, Thought*, trans. Albert Hofstadter (New York: Harper & Row, 1971), 204.—Trans.]

5. [Heidegger, "Der Weg zur Sprache," *Unterwegs*, 244; Hertz, "The Way to Language," *On the Way to Language*, 134.—Trans.]

6. [Again, I have remained closer to Lefebvre's French than to Celan's German.—Trans.]

7. [From the poem "Mit allen Gedanken," *GW* 1: 221; "With all my thoughts," Hamburger, *Celan*, 167.—Trans.]

8. [Celan, "Sprachgitter," *GW* 1: 167; Hamburger, "Language Mesh," *Celan*, 119.—Trans.]

9. [Celan, "Engführung," *GW* 1: 195; Hamburger, "The Straitening," *Celan*, 137.—Trans.]

10. [Celan, "Schneebett," *GW* 1: 168; Hamburger, "Snow-bed," *Celan*, 121.—Trans.]

11. ["Tübingen, Jänner"; Blanchot's French translation is "yeux que la parole submerge jusqu'à la cécité."—Trans.]

12. [Celan, "Schneebett," *GW* 1: 168; Hamburger, "Snow-bed," *Celan*, 121.—Trans.]

13. [From ibid.:

> Augen weltblind,
> Augen im Sterbegeklüft,
> Augen Augen . . .

From "Engführung" (note 9, above):

> Lies nicht mehr—schau!
> Schau nicht mehr—geh!

Lacoue-Labarthe cites the French translation by Maurice Blanchot, "Le dernier à parler," 15.—Trans.]

Ecstasy

1. [Jean-Jacques Rousseau, *Oeuvres complètes*, vol. 1 (Paris: Gallimard, Bibliothèque de la Pléiade, 1959), 1005; *Reveries of the Solitary Walker*, trans. Peter France (Harmondsworth, England: Penguin, 1979), 39.—Trans.]

Vertigo

1. Paris: Hachette/POL, 1979.
2. [*GW* 3: 200.—Trans.]
3. [Du Bouchet, *Strette*.—Trans.]
4. [Jean Launay, "Le Méridien," *Po&sie* 9 (1979): 80.—Trans.]

Blindness

1. [*GW* 1: 274; Hamburger, *Celan*, 211.—Trans.]

Lied

1. [This passage can be found in the afterword to the essay "Das Ding," *Vorträge und Aufsätze*, 183; trans. Hofstadter, *Poetry, Language, Thought*, 164.—Trans.]
2. [Celan, "Zürich, Zum Storchen," *GW* 1: 214; Hamburger, "Zürich, the Stork Inn," *Celan*, 157.—Trans.]
3. The manuscript is dated April 17, 1977.
4. Heidegger's response to Celan on receipt of "Todtnauberg." Altmann mentions at the beginning of his article that this letter, along with the poem itself, had been exhibited in 1970 at Raduz in the exhibition on Celan.
5. The French translation of this text is in large part due to Jean-Luc Nancy, the intermediary between W.H. and me. [The English version has been translated from the French.—Trans.]

Sky

1. [*GW* 3: 108; Washburn and Guillemin, *Last Poems*, 189.—Trans.]
2. [Hölderlin, *SW* 5: 285.—Trans.]
3. [*SW* 2.1: 118; Hamburger, *Friedrich Hölderlin, Poems and Fragments*, 373.—Trans.]
4. Martin Heidegger, "Wie Wenn am Feiertage . . . ," in *Erläuterungen zu Hölderlins Dichtung*, 62.
5. Heidegger, "Das Gedicht," *Erläuterungen*, 187.
6. [Heidegger, *Vorträge und Aufsätze*, 187–204; Hofstadter, *Poetry, Language, Thought*, 213–29.—Trans.]
7. "Kindness" translates *Freundlichkeit*, which Heidegger interprets as the Greek χάρις: grace.
8. [This line in German is "Voll Verdienst," which Michael Hamburger translates as "Full of profit." The French version L.-L. discusses uses "Plein de mérites"; I have modified the English to enhance the sense of L.-L.'s subsequent remarks.—Trans.]
9. [*SW* 2.1: 372; Hamburger, *Hölderlin*, 261–65.—Trans.]
10. [Hofstadter translates: "Is he manifest like the sky?" Hölderlin answers: "I'd sooner believe the latter." The translation here has been modified in accordance with Hofstadter's.—Trans.]
11. [Heidegger, " . . . dichterisch wohnet der Mensch . . . ," *Vorträge und Aufsätze*, 197; Hofstadter, " . . . Poetically Man Dwells . . . ," *Poetry, Language, Thought*, 222–23.—Trans.]
12. In "In Lovely Blueness," these "qualities" are the night stars. About "the shade of the night," Heidegger says: " . . . the night itself is the shade, that darkness which can never become a mere blackness because as shade it is wedded to light and remains cast by it (Heidegger, " . . . dichterisch wohnet der Mensch . . . ," 201; Hofstadter, " . . . Poetically Man Dwells . . . ," 226.)
13. Hölderlin's poem says:

> Was ist Gott? unbekannt, dennoch
> Voll Eigenschaften ist das Angesicht
> Des Himmels von ihm. Die Blitze nämlich
> Der Zorn sind eines Gottes. Jemehr ist eins
> Unsichtbar, schicket es sich in Fremdes.
>
> (*SW* 2.1: 210)
>
> What is God? Unknown, yet
> Full of his qualities is the

Face of the sky. For the lightnings
Are the wrath of a god. The more something
Is invisible, the more it yields to what's alien.

(Hofstadter, 225)

Heidegger's commentary: "The sight of the sky—this is what is familiar to man. And what is that? Everything that shimmers and blooms in the sky and thus under the sky and thus on earth, everything that sounds and is fragrant, rises and comes—but also everything that goes and stumbles, moans and falls silent, pales and darkens. Into this, which is intimate to man but alien to the god, the unknown imparts himself, in order to remain guarded within it as the unknown" ("dichterisch wohnet der Mensch . . . ," 200; Hofstadter, " . . . Poetically Man Dwells . . . ," 225).

14. [Heidegger, " . . . dichterisch wohnet der Mensch . . . ," 200; Hofstadter, " . . . Poetically Man Dwells . . . ," 225.—Trans.]

15. Heidegger, " . . . dichterisch wohnet der Mensch . . . ," 200–201; Hofstadter, " . . . Poetically Man Dwells . . . ," 225–26.

16. See Jean-Luc Marion's reading of the poem in *L'idole et la distance* (Paris: Grasset, 1978).

17. [*SW*, 2.1: 372; Hamburger, *Hölderlin*, 261.—Trans.]

18. [*GW* 1: 163; Hamburger, *Celan*, 113.—Trans.]

Works Cited

Adorno, Theodor. *Notes to Literature.* Vol. 2. Trans. Shierry Weber Nicholson. New York: Columbia University Press, 1991.

Allemann, Beda. *Hölderlin et Heidegger.* Paris: P.U.F., 1959.

Beaufret, Jean, trans. "Hölderlin et Sophocle." In Friedrich Hölderlin, *Remarques sur Oedipe-Remarques sur Antigone.* Paris: U.G.E., 1965.

Benjamin, Walter. *Charles Baudelaire: A Lyric Poet in the Era of High Capitalism.* Trans. Harry Zohn. London: NLB, 1973.

———. *Gesammelte Schriften.* 7 vols. Ed. Rolf Tiedemann and Hermann Schweppenhäuser. Frankfurt am Main: Suhrkamp, 1974.

———. *Illuminations.* Ed. Hannah Arendt. Trans. Harry Zohn. New York: Schocken, 1969.

———. *Reflections.* Ed. Peter Demetz. Trans. Edmund Jephcott. New York: Schocken, 1986.

Blanchot, Maurice. "Le dernier à parler." *La revue des belles lettres* 2 (1972); this essay was reissued as a single text. Paris: fata morgana, 1984.

Bonargent, René. *Tournoyer.*

Böschenstein, Bernard. "Destitutions." *La revue des belles lettres* 2 (1972).

Büchner, Georg. *Dantons Tod.* In *Werke und Briefe,* ed. Fritz Bergemann. Wiesbaden: Insel, 1949.

———. *The Death of Danton.* Trans. Howard Brenton and Jane Fry. In *The Complete Plays,* ed. Michael Patterson. London: Methuen, 1987.

———. *Leonce and Lena.* In *Complete Works and Letters,* trans. Henry J. Schmidt. New York: Continuum, 1986.

Celan, Paul. *Gesammelte Werke.* 5 vols. Ed. Beda Allemann and Stefan Reichert, with Rolf Bücher. Frankfurt: Suhrkamp, 1983.

———. *Last Poems: Paul Celan.* Trans. Katharine Washburn and Margret Guillemin. San Francisco: North Point, 1986.

———. "Le Méridien." In *Strette,* trans. André du Bouchet. Paris: Mercure de France, 1971.

———. "'Le Méridien.' Discours prononcé à l'occasion de la remise du prix Georg Büchner." Trans. Jean Launay. *Poǽsie* 9 (1979): 68–82.

———. "The Meridian." Trans. Jerry Glenn. *Chicago Review* 29, no. 3 (1978): 29–40.

———. *Paul Celan: Collected Prose.* Trans. Rosmarie Waldrop. Manchester, England: Carcanet Press, 1986.

———. *Poems of Paul Celan.* Trans. Michael Hamburger. New York: Persea, 1988.

———. *Paul Celan: 65 Poems.* Trans. Brian Lynch and Peter Jankowsky. Dublin: Raven Arts, 1985.

———. *Paul Celan: Speech-Grille and Selected Poems.* Trans. Joachim Neugroschel. New York: E.P. Dutton, 1971.

———. *La rose de personne.* Ed. Martine Broda. Paris: Le Nouveau Commerce, 1979.

———. "Todtnauberg." In *Poèmes de Paul Celan,* trans. André du Bouchet. Paris: Clivages, 1978.

———. "Tübingen, janvier." Trans. André du Bouchet. In *L'Ephémère* 7. Also published in *Strette.* Paris: Mercure de France, 1971.

Derrida, Jacques. "Pas (préambule)." *Gramma* 3-4 (1976). Reprinted in Derrida, *Parages,* 19–116. Paris: Galilée, 1986.

Friedell, Egon. *Talents zur Wahrheit,* 1910.

Hamacher, Werner. "The Second of Inversion: Movements of a Figure Through Celan's Poetry." Trans. Peter Fenves. In *Word Traces: Readings of Paul Celan,* ed. Aris Fioretos, 219–63. Baltimore, Md.: Johns Hopkins University Press, 1994.

Heidegger, Martin. *Die Erfahrung des Denkens.* Frankfurt: Klostermann, 1983.

———. *Einführung in die Metaphysik.* Tübingen: Niemeyer, 1953.

———. *Erläuterungen zu Hölderlins Dichtung.* Frankfurt: Klostermann, 1981.

———. *Gesamtausgabe.* Frankfurt: Klostermann, 1976–.

———. *Hölderlins Hymne "Der Ister."* Frankfurt: Klostermann, 1984.

———. *Holzwege.* Frankfurt: Klostermann, 1950.

————. *On the Way to Language.* Trans. Peter D. Hertz. San Francisco: Harper & Row, 1971.

————. *Poetry, Language, Thought.* Trans. Albert Hofstadter. New York: Harper & Row, 1971.

————. *The Principle of Reason.* Trans. Reginald Lilly. Bloomington: Indiana University Press, 1991.

————. *Satz vom Grund.* Pfullingen: Neske, 1957.

————. *Sein und Zeit.* 11th ed. Tübingen: Niemeyer, 1967.

————. *Unterwegs zur Sprache.* Frankfurt: Klostermann, 1985.

————. *Vorträge und Aufsätze.* Pfullingen: Neske, 1954.

————. *Wegmarken.* Frankfurt: Klostermann, 1967.

————. *Zur Sache des Denkens.* Tübingen: Niemeyer, 1969.

Heraclitus. *Die Fragmente der Vorsokratiker.* 5th ed. Trans. Hermann Diels. Ed. Walther Kranz. Berlin: Weidmann, 1934.

Hölderlin, Friedrich. *Friedrich Hölderlin: Essays and Letters on Theory.* Trans. Thomas Pfau. Albany: SUNY Press, 1988.

————. *Friedrich Hölderlin: Poems and Fragments.* Trans. Michael Hamburger. Cambridge: Cambridge University Press, 1980.

————. *Hymns and Fragments.* Trans. Richard Sieburth. Princeton, N.J.: Princeton University Press, 1984.

————. *Hölderlin: His Poems.* Trans. Michael Hamburger. New York: Pantheon, 1952.

————. *Sämtliche Werke.* 8 vols. Stuttgart: Kohlhammer, 1944–85.

Kafka, Franz. "Ein Bericht für eine Akademie." In *Gesammelte Werke in sieben Bänden.* Frankfurt: Hanser, 1983.

Lacoue-Labarthe, Philippe. "La césure du spéculatif." In Friedrich Hölderlin, *L'Antigone de Sophocle.* Trans. Philippe Lacoue-Labarthe. Paris: Bourgois, 1978.

————. "Hölderlin et les Grecs." *Poétique* 40 (1979).

————. *Mimesis désarticulations.* Paris: Aubier-Flammarion, 1975.

————. *Typography: Mimesis, Philosophy, Politics.* Ed. Christopher Fynsk. Cambridge: Harvard University Press, 1989.

Launay, Jean. "Une lecture de Paul Celan." *Po&sie* 9 (1979): 3–8.

Lévinas, Emmanuel. *Autrement qu'être ou au-delà de l'essence.* Haag: Nijhoff, 1974.

————. "De l'être à l'autre." *La revue des belles lettres* 3 (1972).

Marion, Jean-Luc. *L'idole et la distance.* Paris: Grasset, 1978.

Meschonnic, Henri. *Pour la poétique II.* Paris: Gallimard, 1980.

Munier, Roger. Essay in *Mise en page* 1 (May 1972).

Nancy, Jean-Luc. *Le discours de la syncope*. Paris: Aubier-Flammarion, 1976.

Rimbaud, Arthur. *Oeuvres II: Vers nouveaux, Une saison en enfer*. Paris: Garnier-Flammarion, 1989.

———. *Rimbaud: Complete Works, Selected Letters*. Trans. Wallace Fowlie. Chicago: University of Chicago Press, 1966.

Rousseau, Jean-Jacques. *Oeuvres complètes*. Vol. 1. Paris: Gallimard, Bibliothèque de la Pléïade, 1959.

———. *Reveries of the Solitary Walker*. Trans. Peter France. Harmondsworth, England: Penguin, 1979.

Szondi, Peter. "Eden." In *Poésies et poétiques de la modernité*. Lille: Presses Universitaires de Lille, 1981.

MERIDIAN

Crossing Aesthetics

Deborah Esch, *In the Event: Reading Journalism, Reading Theory*

Winfried Menninghaus, *In Praise of Nonsense: Kant and Bluebeard*

Giorgio Agamben, *The Man Without Content*

Giorgio Agamben, *The End of the Poem: Essays in Poetics*

Theodor W. Adorno, *Sound Figures*

Louis Marin, *Sublime Poussin*

Philippe Lacoue-Labarthe, *Poetry as Experience*

Jacques Derrida, *Resistances of Psychoanalysis*

Ernst Bloch, *Literary Essays*

Marc Froment-Meurice, *That Is to Say: Heidegger's Poetics*

Francis Ponge, *Soap*

Philippe Lacoue-Labarthe, *Typography: Mimesis, Philosophy, Politics*

Giorgio Agamben, *Homo Sacer: Sovereign Power and Bare Life*

Emmanuel Levinas, *Of God Who Comes to Mind*

Bernard Stiegler, *Technics and Time, 1: The Fault of Epimetheus*

Werner Hamacher, *pleroma—Reading in Hegel*

Serge Leclaire, *Psychoanalyzing: On the Order of the Unconscious and the Practice of the Letter*

Serge Leclaire, *A Child Is Being Killed: On Primary Narcissism and the Death Drive*

Sigmund Freud, *Writings on Art and Literature*

Cornelius Castoriadis, *World in Fragments: Writings on Politics, Society, Psychoanalysis, and the Imagination*

Thomas Keenan, *Fables of Responsibility: Aberrations and Predicaments in Ethics and Politics*

Emmanuel Levinas, *Proper Names*

Alexander García Düttmann, *At Odds with AIDS: Thinking and Talking About a Virus*

Maurice Blanchot, *Friendship*

Jean-Luc Nancy, *The Muses*

Massimo Cacciari, *Posthumous People: Vienna at the Turning Point*

David E. Wellbery, *The Specular Moment: Goethe's Early Lyric and the Beginnings of Romanticism*

Edmond Jabès, *The Little Book of Unsuspected Subversion*

Hans-Jost Frey, *Studies in Poetic Discourse: Mallarmé, Baudelaire, Rimbaud, Hölderlin*

Pierre Bourdieu, *The Rules of Art: Genesis and Structure of the Literary Field*

Nicolas Abraham, *Rhythms: On the Work, Translation, and Psychoanalysis*

Jacques Derrida, *On the Name*

David Wills, *Prosthesis*

Maurice Blanchot, *The Work of Fire*

Jacques Derrida, *Points . . . : Interviews, 1974–1994*